For ages an endeavor simply ignored and for decades a calling held in contempt, the study of popular culture has in our time been coming of age. For this, we can thank scholars such as Professor Lohof. In this volume he discusses some aspects of American popular culture: advertising and celebrities, architecture, short fiction and magazines, the academy. Professor Lohof analyzes these subjects with a variety of methodological approaches: the myth/image movement; the literature of sociology, structuralist theory and statistical content analysis.

American Commonplace

American
Commonplace
Essays on the Popular Culture of the United States

Bruce Lohof

Bowling Green State University Popular Press
Bowling Green, Ohio 43403

Library of Congress Catalog Card No.: 82-73977

ISBN: 0-87972-221-5 Clothbound
      0-87972-222-3 Paperback

Acknowledgements:

Portions of this book have appeared in different form in *Centennial Review, Industrial Archaeology, Industrial Archaeology Review, Journal of Popular Culture,* or *Popular Music and Society.*

DEDICATION

My hands are
my Mother's
becoming
my Father's

An intellectual is a person who can listen to the William Tell overture and not think of the Lone Ranger.

—A.W.L.

Contents

Foreword:
The Purpose of the Book

*F*or ages an endeavor simply ignored and for decades a calling held in contempt, the study of popular culture has in our time been coming of age. It is indeed curious that American popular culture should for so long have been an area of darkness among American academics, for its elements, all and each of them are an American commonplace. They are evidences and examples of the everywhere culture that has come to characterize our time and place.

In the pages that follow I have tried to understand a few such commonplace artifacts of life in modern America: advertising and celebrities, architecture, short fiction and magazines, the academy. It is not a nascent road that I have traveled, but I have nevertheless tried in the essays that follow to contribute in at least two ways to popular culture studies in the United States. First I have been at pains to range away from the topics that have dominated popular culture scholarship in America, particularly fiction and cinema, to examine other and I think equally important subjects. And second I have endeavored to inform my analyses of these newer subjects with the variety of methodological approaches that, if seldom employed by popular culturists, is nevertheless applicable to the study of popular culture.

Thus in chapter one I have adopted the myth/image techniques that so long dominated the American studies movement to examine the largest single fact of our semantic environment: advertising. We have always known that advertising goes beyond the mere informing of consumers to their enticement and manipulation, but in utilizing techniques developed by Henry Nash Smith and Leo Marx and others we can begin to understand the advertiser's most manipulative enticement: the merchandised metaphor. In chapter two I have been interested in merchandise of a different sort: the celebrity. Specifically I have wanted to know why celebrities of the moment appear so strikingly similar to heroes of the ages, for it is a hero that we so often crave and a celebrity that we usually celebrate. And in this endeavor I have chosen to be instructed by the literature of sociology, believing as I do that celebrities are overwhelmingly sociological phenomena.

Popular architecture is everywhere in our lives but seldom in our popular culture studies. Therefore in both the third and fourth chapters I have examined gasoline service stations and fast-food restaurants and I trust by implication other examples of what I have joined John A. Kouwenhoven in calling the vernacular in American architecture. Though to my knowledge they were not overly concerned with architecture in this literal sense, my own thoughts on the matter have been profoundly affected by the structuralist thinking of the famous Frenchman Claude Levi-Strauss and the less famous but equally seminal Russian Vladimir Propp. And if these structuralist theoreticians have been but silently instructive in chapters three and four their ideas are on overt display in the fifth chapter. Here I have attempted my most rigorous application of structuralism's principles to a genre of popular fiction both omnipresent in and uniquely suited to the so-called women's magazines: the short short story.

Chapter six is the result of a statistical content analysis of *Playboy* performed, as I have shown, at the moment of the magazine's curious politization. Though usually honored in breach, the strategies of the content analysts are useful for popular culturists because they lend the hand of objectivity to the enormous samples with which they must effectively deal. For me at any rate content analysis has led to some rather unorthodox conclusions regarding America's eleventh largest and most notorious monthly periodical.

And finally in chapter seven I have returned to the campus to assess the impact of popular culture on the academy itself. As I have shown, though he is no longer with us, Marshall McLuhan and the popular culture that he explained to us has had a profound impact on the life and thinking of men and women who have held themselves quite immune from such matters.

If I have in fact applied the lesser used strategies to the lesser studied subjects, the applications and observations have been my own. And yet so many persons have contributed to my understanding of these things that I cannot but mention a few of them. It began with Gerry Critoph and John Hague at Stetson University and continued with Nelson Blake at Syracuse. Colleagues and students at both Heidelberg College and the University of Miami have been instructive and helpful, chief among them Ben Berry and George Chillag, Ken Davison and Leslie Fishel, Ray O'Connor, Linna-Margaret Place and Phyllis Salesky. Among colleagues far and wide I have special gratitude for John Cawelti, Marshall Fishwick, Henry Glassie, Russel Nye, Isaac Sequira, and above all for Ray Browne, the doyen of popular culture studies and my good friend.

Portions of this book have appeared in different form in *Centennial Review, Industrial Archaeology, Industrial Archaeology Review, Journal of Popular Culture,* or *Popular Music and Society,* and I am grateful to the editors of those journals for earlier hearings given to my work. And finally, as I have learned the hard way that no culture can be understood from within, my warm regards are extended to the two institutions that have allowed me to see America from afar. I speak of course of the American Studies Research Centre in Hyderabad, India, and the United States Educational Foundation in Pakistan.

Bruce Lohof

Islamabad
1983

One

Advertisement: The Higher Meaning of Marlboro Cigarettes

In 1960 S. I. Hayakawa, lately of the United States Senate but then a respected semanticist, delivered a lecture in which he related a personal and homely anecdote surrounding the birth of the Hayakawas' first child:

> I was kind of thrilled and excited [he confessed], and so I wrote a poem about it. After it was written my wife pointed out to me:
> "It's a very nice poem, but you can't sell it."
> "Why not?" I asked.
> "Well, Pet Milk and Gerber's Food have taken over those emotions for commercial purposes."

Another reading of the poem told Hayakawa that it was straight copy for a baby lotion advertisement. "All the baby food suppliers, the diaper services, and so on," he realized, were "exploiting the hell out of mother love for purposes of sale of products."[1]

This technique of exploitation—Hayakawa called it the "poeticizing of consumer goods"—is of course not peculiar to the mother-love industries. Elemental in much effective advertising is the transubstantiation of soup or beer or laxatives into symbols of some higher good. Thus in the 1920s lip rouge was no mere cosmetic but a symbol of sexuality: "It's comforting to know," assured the commercial pages of *Ladies' Home Journal*, "that the alluring note of scarlet will stay with you for hours." Thus in the 1960s the once humdrum soft drink Pepsi Cola became the potation of an entire generation of youthful and vigorous funseekers. The Pepsi Generation, they were:

5

> ... comin' at ya, goin' strong;
> Put yourself behind a Pepsi,
> If you're livin', you belong.

Thus in the age of OPEC people delight in snubbing symbols of automotive hauteur and extravagance—Cadillac or Mercedes Benz—and once you "get your hands on a Toyota, you'll never let go!"

The 1920s were an era of new sexual freedom and the Scarlet Woman's rouge was therefore worth wearing. In its promise of youth the Pepsi Generation had antecedents at least as old as Ponce de Leon's search for the Fountain. And is there not a certain civic responsibility that cloaks every owner of a small, efficient automobile? But there is a breed of advertising that transcends the consumer's itch for sex, youth, or status. The more perceptive of Madison Avenue's moguls sell products by identifying them with what the critic Leo Marx called a "cultural symbol," by which he meant "an image that conveys a special meaning (thought and feeling) to. . . [the] large number of people who share the culture" with, in this case, the advertiser and the product.[2] This transcendent form of advertising offers to consumers an image that will evoke a cluster of ideas and emotions which they hold in common with their fellow Americans. It is not simply soap or soft drinks that are for sale. It is not even sex or security. Rather it is the *merchandising of a metaphor* that will speak to and be understood by the collective imagination of the culture.

Doubtless the finest American example of the merchandised metaphor is the Marlboro Man who since 1963 has been emblematic of Marlboro Cigarettes. Rugged, vigorous and robust, he has stridden through the media: crouching before a daybreak fire to turn the crinkling bacon or pour coffee from a blackened pot, riding his horse across the upland country, or participating in the annual roundup. In every case he is lighting up, and suggesting that you follow his lead. He is to be sure the consummate cowboy. But he is much more.

The Marlboro Men.
Courtesy Philip Morris Company.

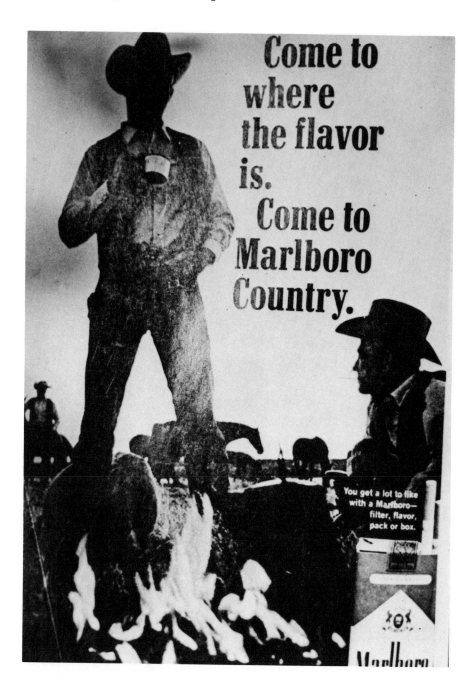

Marlboro's Tattooed Man.

Courtesy Philip Morris Company.

The Marlboro Man.
Courtesy Philip Morris Company

There was a time however when he was not a cowboy at all. For three decades the person in the Marlboro advertisement had as often as not been a lady, and invariably in plush, upholstered surroundings. Marlboro Cigarettes in the days before the Marlboro Man had been "America's luxury cigarette," a genteel smoke available with either an "ivory tip" or a red "beauty tip." And the affluent, textured salons in which they were smoked connoted a deep-pile luxury and velvet sophistication that bordered on the effeminate. Indeed Marlboros were widely regarded as a lady's smoke forty years before another brand, Virginia Slims, began the fatuous congratulations of the American woman on having come:

> ... a long way, baby,
> To get where you've got to today;
> You've got your own cigaret, now, baby;
> You've come a long, long way.

Then the 1950s brought the first cancer scare and the scare in turn brought a bromide: cigarette filters. A spate of filtered brands entered the market, among them the Philip Morris Company's early bid. "New from Philip Morris," the slogan said, and Americans discovered that Marlboros, an old brand in new clothing, now had a "filter, flavor, [and a] fliptop box." Moreover lest the effeminacy of old be augmented by sissiness that plagued the earliest filtered cigarettes, Marlboro was given a new, masculine image: the tattooed man.

By chance the first tattooed man was a cowboy. No Marlboro Man, he was simply the result of the advertisers' desire to identify their product with "regular guys." As an agency executive later recalled: "We asked ourselves what was the most genuinely accepted symbol of masculinity in America, and this led quite naturally to a cowboy." Apparently no effort was made to transform this initial cowboy into the cultural symbol that would eventually emerge. Indeed, the tattooed man soon forsook the range in

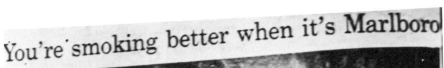

The Marlboro Face.

Courtesy Philip Morris Company.

pursuit of other manly vocations. "Obviously," advertisers erroneously reasoned, "we couldn't keep on showing cowboys forever, although they could be repeated from time to time." In his place came a succession of heroes: explorers, sailors, athletes and an occasional tuxedoed but no less rugged gentleman. In each case the common denominator was an elemental masculinity and of course the tattoo, emblem of those who look "successful and sophisticated but rugged...as though [they] might have had interesting experiences."[3]

But the tattooed man, like the imagination of the culture that smoked his cigarettes, kept returning to the open range of his birth. His Madison Avenue creators had meant for him to wear cowboy regalia only on occasion, but the costume was becoming his natural clothing. In the early '60s the cowboy was promoted to supremacy over other tattooed men; by 1963 the tattoo itself had disappeared and the cowboy emerged as the exclusive inhabitant of Marlboro Cigarette advertisements. A cultural symbol had been discovered; a metaphor was ready to be merchandised.

The Marlboro image, though woven into whole cloth, consists of two elements, each of which is illuminated in the neon of advertising slogans. One naturally is the Marlboro Man himself. The other is what the popular culture scholar John Cawelti has called the "symbolic landscape," the element of the larger Western myth that so influences "the character and actions of the hero."[4] And for our hero the Marlboro Man, the symbolic landscape is nicely expressed in the phrase: "Come to Marlboro Country."

Marlboro Country in a sense is Montana, the Montana that once so astounded that Eastern, erudite Jew Leslie Fiedler. "The inhumanly virginal landscape: the atrocious magnificence of the mountains, the illimitable brute fact of the prairies": this is Marlboro Country. It is, as the license plates say, the "Big Sky Country." Had it not been for Rousseau's romantic myth of noble savagery, Fiedler admitted, he would have been psychologically impotent in the face of its virginal enormity. He would have had no way of comprehending it; there would have been nothing for him "to do with it...no way of assimilating the land to [his] imagination."[5]

But the Rousseauean legacy has enjoyed a succession of able trustees: Natty Bumppo and Daniel Boone, Manifest Destiny and the Spirit of '49, a generation of dime novelists and another of Hollywood cowboys. The list goes on. Thus has the symbolic landscape of Marlboro Country been made not only mentally manageable but psychologically fascinating. What might have boggled the national mind by its sheer immensity in fact evokes within the cultural consciousness a nostalgic and reverent image of its own mythical heritage. Marlboro Country is an environmental memoir, reminding Americans of where they like to believe they once lived and inviting them to return.

At first glance Marlboro Country is reminiscent of the Vergilian pastoral ideal. Folded, spindled and mutilated, modern Americans might view the Marlboro Man's vernal expanses with the envy of Vergil's exiled shepherd:

> ... while you lie there at ease under the awning of a spreading beech and practice country songs... I have to bid good-bye to the home fields and the ploughlands that I love. Exile for me... and you lie sprawling in the shade, teaching the woods to echo back the charms of Amaryllis.

Indeed the rustic garden is a potent force in the American mind. As Marx showed, the intrusion of "technology" into the "pastoral ideal"—or to use his title *The Machine in the Garden*—is a "metaphoric design which recurs everywhere in our literature" from James Fenimore Cooper and Washington Irving to Ernest Hemingway and Robert Frost.[6] So envious are urbanized Americans of the pastoral ideal that it spills out of their elite art and across their commercial advertising. Thus once the consumer realizes that "You can take Salem out of the country, but you can't take the 'Country' out of Salem" he and some modern Amaryllis are only a pack of smokes away from a gambol through a field of waving grass toward a shadowy glade. Here Rip Van Winkle escaped from the village to a cozy repose in the midst of tranquil nature. Here Henry David Thoreau escaped Boston and even Concord to the benign shores of Walden Pond. Here also menthol-puffing couples meander barefoot across an oaken bridge with never a thought of splinters. Here picnics are antless, and summers are both sweatless and endless, which is to say winterless. Here one can find pleasant refuge from the responsibilities and encumbrances of civilization.* But the trill of shepherds' pipes and the wooded serenity of a Hollywood back lot are upon closer inspection aliens in Marlboro Country. They belong instead to the pastoral verdure of Arcadia, that middle landscape that edges upon civilization. On the nether edge of Arcadia however is the wilderness: primitive, violent, perhaps even malevolent. This is the incredible landscape of Fiedler's Montana. This is the monstrous and illimitable home of the noble savage. This is Marlboro Country.

The cursory distinctions between the garden and the wilderness are aesthetic. They are the bucolic greenery of eternal summer versus the rough-hewn realism of the Frederick Remington paintings that have occasionally been used in Marlboro advertisements. And prior to 1971—when commercials for tobacco products were banned from the air—they were the capricious flutes of the shepherd versus the strident, robust brass of *The Magnificent Seven,* the classic Western motion picture whose virile musical theme

---

*As counterpart to these observations it is interesting to note that in the 1970s Salem Cigarette advertisements increasingly came to be located on a remote sea island rather than in a woody glade. This movement toward American culture's other great metaphoric design, the lure of the sea, has perhaps been typified best in the "gusto" commercials and advertisements for Schlitz Beer. In its potency as a cultural symbol among Americans only the lure of the sea matches the lure of the West.

accompanied every Marlboro television and radio
commercial. Beneath the surface though lie more critical
differences. The pastoral ideal promises a benign nature free
of conflict, danger and tension. The primitive ideal speaks
on the other hand of a wilderness that confronts and
jeopardizes its denizens. Accordingly the Vergilian
shepherd lies in repose, unharassed by the complicated
tensions of the town, safe from the forbidding dangers of the
marsh.[7] In contrast his wilderness counterpart stands erect
and vigilant. A man in conflict with his landscape, he is of
necessity a man of purpose and action. He is the Marlboro
Man.

The Marlboro Man personifies the awesome and
primitive landscape in which he lives. His clothing reflects
the competitive spirit that is exacted by the wilderness. His
attire is not the spangled costume of dime-store Texans and
back-lot cowboys, nor is it the casual drape of the classic
shepherd. Rather he wears a rough-spun shirt, sheepskin
vest or coat, dungarees and chaps. Nothing is for show, and
little is for comfort; everything is for facing down the
elements. And his habits like his clothing are dictated by
practical considerations. In the days before the television
ban the musical jingle always had him "Up before the sun,
Travel[ing] all day long," and each commercial presented
another workaday vignette: rescuing a stranded herd from
the snowbound uplands, mending fence, rounding up stray
calves, thwarting an incipient stampede. Even his leisure
moments—gathering water for the morning coffee or
competing in the local rodeo—are reflections of his real
purposes. His habits are work-oriented, his work a way of
life.

But the essence of the Marlboro Man, whether the
medium be thirty seconds of air time or a back cover in four-
color print, is found in his countenance. His face does not
reflect the placid serenity of the shepherd. Nor does it mirror
either the cosmetic polish of civilization's winners or the
sullen weariness worn by its victims. Like his clothing and
his habits, the countenance of the Marlboro Man comes with

The Marlboro face.
Courtesy Philip Morris Company

the territory: sculptured, cragged, lined not by age but by the elements. Suitably he gazes out upon Marlboro Country through what Fiedler called the " 'Montana Face'... a face developed not for sociability or feeling, but for facing into the weather."[8] A rude sagaciousness of eye, a leathery tautness of skin, a wind-cured ruddiness of complexion—altogether a rugged handsomeness—perfectly connote his sturdy lifestyle.

The higher meaning of Marlboro Cigarettes in fine cannot be written in terms of tobacco or even of mere machismo. Not cigarettes, not even manhood, but an entire metaphor is here being merchandised. The Marlboro image is a cultural symbol that, to paraphrase Marx, speaks to the collective imagination of the American people. It speaks of the virgin frontier, and of the brutal efficiency and constant vigilance which that frontier expects from its people. It speaks, as did the historian Frederick Jackson Turner nearly a century ago, of the American frontier's insistence on a:

> coarseness and strength combined with acuteness and inquisitiveness; that practical, inventive turn of mind, quick to find expedients; that masterful grasp of material things, lacking in the artistic but powerful to effect great ends; that restless, nervous energy; that dominant individualism, working for good and for evil, and withal that buoyancy and exuberance which comes with freedom....[9]

In short the Marlboro image speaks of *innocence* and of individual *efficacy*: innocence in spite of the Marlboro Man's rude sagacity, efficacy because the landscape has determined that as the price of survival. It was the innocence of the Marlboro Man which prompted Fiedler to write that in Montana "there was something heartening in dealing with people who had never seen... a Negro or a Jew or a Servant, and were immune to all their bitter meanings."[10] Similarly in Marlboro Country, we are led to believe, one finds a breed of humanity untarnished by the acrid fumes of civilization. His naivete is as fresh as the unpolluted air that he breathes, as pure as the mountain stream which quenches his thirst. In the countenance of the Marlboro Man there is not the mingled guilt and terror that flickers in the civilized eye whenever it sees a ghetto or a mushroom cloud or a riot. He represents a reprieve from the malaise that hangs darkly over all who have become accessories to the crimes of civilization.

The Marlboro image however is not evocative of simple escape. To be sure the Marlboro Man stands apart from civilization, but he stands apart also from Arcadia, from the simple, purposeless, unencumbered dawdling of Salem Country. Like the city and unlike the Vergilian garden, Marlboro Country makes demands upon its denizens. But problems there can be solved; the tasks require vigilance, rigor and diligence, but the rewards are resolution and accomplishment. Possessed of those virtues that Turner memorialized—"that practical, inventive turn of mind... that masterful grasp of material things"—the Marlboro Man is "powerful to effect great ends."

The symbol at work here represents escape not from the responsibilities of civilization so much as from its frustrations. Most moderns wallow through encumbrances so tangled, bureaucracies so entwined, and institutions so sinuous that the reward is usually impotence and desperation. Responsible for nothing, unfulfilled in everything, can they help but be drawn to the Marlboro Man as he faces down his challenge? He lives as we all would live, as Thoreau's *Walden* would have had us live: "deliberately... front[ing] only the essential facts of life."

Innocence and efficacy are the touchstones of the Marlboro metaphor. Of course Marlboro Country has itself become a victim of technology, as have the virtues which it nourished. Curiously however technology has a way of reconstituting the shadow of that which it has destroyed. So it is with the Marlboro Man, his habits and appearance, his landscape, his virtues: a way of life which became a folk myth in the minds of a people is once again conjured into "reality," this time for commercial purposes. Early in the cowboy's Marlboro career the editor of a trade journal questioned the "intrusion" of cowboys "into... advertising— as authorities on cigarets, bourbon, and automobiles." Noting the cowboy's alleged penchant "for personal ornamentation, preening, drinking and brawling," his presumed tendency toward "regarding females largely in the herd," and the notorious aroma "of horses, dung and sweaty saddle leather" that follows wherever he goes, the editor thought it paradoxical that "civilized advertising men can parade him before us as someone whose habits are worthy of copying." Of course the answer to the editor's paradox is that the Marlboro Man is not simply a cowboy, but has a higher meaning. He is a symbol of irretrievable innocence and of that illimitable wilderness wherein, as Emerson said in his *Journals*, we might once have been "plain old Adam, the simple genuine self against the whole world."

Two

Celebrity:
The Rise and Fall of Burt Bacharach

The story is told that in 1943 Burt Bacharach, then a lad of fifteen years, was whistling a tune while a Manhatten bus carried him to his next piano lesson.

"Is that 'The Two O'Clock Jump'?" asked a young man seated beside him. He was, it turned out, Leonard Bernstein, then assistant conductor of the New York Philharmonic Orchestra.

"I've never heard of you," said the callow Bacharach, but the two young musicians chatted for a while. And when the bus rolled up to Burt's stop he got off saying: "So long, Lennie, see you at the top."

This pretentious augury of youth in time became prophecy fulfilled. Leonard Bernstein disembarked from that bus to watch the ballerinas twirl to his *Fancy Free*, to listen with millions of others to the music of his Broadway and subsequently Hollywood hit musical *West Side Story*, to see Marlon Brando mumble and stumble to the accompaniment of his score for the classic film *On the Waterfront*. He became a widely televised lecturer and conductor, an ambassador of classical music to the court of little children, and a tousled-headed symbol of a culture that is not only *haut* but good fun as well. Indeed so famous did

21

Bernstein become that he was made the object of an elaborate and equally famous joke in the writer Tom Wolfe's *Radical Chic.*[1] And what of Bacharach? For his part he became a famous composer of popular music. Moreover he became a national idol, serving his brief time as Stephen Foster, Irving Berlin, George Gershwin and Cole Porter served theirs. By his forty-second birthday, he had become, as one news magazine put it in a cover story, "Music Man 1970."[2] And then, just as quickly, he disappeared.

How does a callow lad grow into a Music Man? Composers—the Beatles' Paul McCartney and John Lennon being perhaps the classic examples—must usually sing their own songs if they would themselves become famous. The remainder receive about as much public acclaim as a collection of certified public accountants. How is it then that in this cultural setting Burt Bacharach, tunesmith, would become a national idol? What were the contours of his rise, the causes of his fall? And what does his story tell us about the stuff of celebrities, how they are made and undone?

That Bacharach became a celebrity is hardly open to question. Indeed at the time it seemed that he had assumed even heroic proportions. After all, students of hero-worship had long since charted the genetic processes by which heroes are born and Bacharach's rise to fame had definitely been recollective of the sequence. As early as 1949 the sociologist Orrin Klapp had designated "the main phases of this process...as follows: 1) spontaneous or unorganized popular homage, 2) formal recognition and honor, 3) the building up of an idealized image or legend of the hero, 4) commemoration of the hero, and 5) established cult."[3] A hero, Klapp hastened to add, need not pass through the entire sequence, but the "Music Man 1970" traveled more than half the way:

Popular homage takes a variety of forms. Charles Lindbergh's heroism began at Le Bourget Field in May of 1927 when thousands of Frenchmen dragged him bodily from "The Spirit of St. Louis" and carried him upon their shoulders for nearly a half hour. The heroism of Jack and Bobby Kennedy was born in the frenzied mobs that thronged to touch and see them. The homage paid to athletes and actors is measured at the box office. So also in a manner of speaking was the homage paid to Burt Bacharach: by the time that he was acclaimed "Music Man 1970" the people's pocketbook had turned more than two dozen of his tunes into hit songs.* A single songstress, Dionne Warwick, had sold more than twelve million copies of Bacharach's pieces. One of his songs, "Raindrops Keep Fallin' On My Head," had sold three million recordings and nearly a million copies of sheet music. Bacharach was commanding $35,000 per week for concerts; he owned a lucrative share of the company that produced his recordings and all of the publishing house that sold his music. In a land and calling where popular homage is gauged in dollars, Burt Bacharach was a wealthy man.

Formal recognition and honor came in 1970. In March Bacharach received two "Oscars" from the American Academy of Motion Picture Arts and Sciences, one for the music score of the Western motion picture *Butch Cassidy and the Sundance Kid*, the other for a song from that score, the aforementioned "Raindrops Keep Fallin' On My Head." A month later the National Academy of Recording Arts and

*"Any Day Now," "Tower of Strength," "You're Following Me," "The Man Who Shot Liberty Valance," "Magic Moments," "Don't Make Me Over," "Make it Easy on Yourself," "Only Love Can Break a Heart," "Blue on Blue," "True Love Never Runs Smooth," "24 Hours from Tulsa," "Anyone Who Had A Heart," "Wishin' and Hopin'," "Walk On By," "Reach Out for Me," "I Wake Up Crying'," "Don't Envy Me," "(There's) Always Something There to Remind Me," "Trains and Boats and Planes," "What the World Needs Now is Love," "The Windows of the World," "I Say A Little Prayer," "Raindrops Keep Fallin' On My Head," "I'll Never Fall In Love Again," "Wives and Lovers," "A House Is Not A Home," "Send Me No Flowers," "What's New, Pussycat," and "Alfie."

Sciences awarded him two "Grammies," again one for the score of *Butch Cassidy and the Sundance Kid* and the other for the recorded soundtrack of his Broadway hit musical *Promises, Promises.* This year also saw him in two televised musical extravaganzas simply entitled "An Evening with Burt Bacharach" and "Another Evening with Burt Bacharach," both broadcast by the National Broadcasting Company, both sponsored by America's largest food products company, Kraft.

Following sponataneous homage and formal recognition of Bacharach—and in keeping with Klapp's sequence of hero-development—came the evolution of a Bacharach *image and legend.* The Bacharach of the flesh remained an unknown quantity, of course. True to all public figures, it was doubly true of Bacharach, who as has been mentioned, followed a usually obscure calling.* In the vacuum of public ignorance a consumable Bacharach became necessary, for heroes can be mysterious or enigmatic but never intangible. Moreover what was necessary was also easy, for within the public domain little of the real man existed to erase or contradict.

As a commodity Bacharach was partially image. Erotically handsome, "Burt," Broadway producer David Merrick was alleged to have said, "turned out to be a sex symbol." And in matters both tonsorial and sartorial the 1970s found him impeccably disheveled, studiously unkempt, casually *haut.* The image loomed largest perhaps in his concerts whether live or televised: the calisthenic style of his conducting, complete with karate chops to the percussion section, blurring fingers in the direction of the woodwinds, his body all the while swiveling from one keyboard to another for an appropriate tinkle or a generous progression of chords. Each facet of the image was perhaps best caught in a stop-action portrait that the logotypographers came to use as a signature for his televised

---

*Appropriately throughout Bacharach's days in the limelight his lyricist partner Hal David remained an almost total obscurity.

Burt Bacharach.

concerts. The erotic good looks, the tousled hair and casual clothing, the calisthenics: all of it is there, captured forever like the maiden running across Keats' Grecian urn.

But the consumable Bacharach was also partially legend, and like all legends it adhered to familiarly epic designs. The public nodded in reminiscence of Horatio Alger's Phil the Fiddler when it heard of Bacharach's odyssey through the famous borscht circuit of upstate New York. Working in a Catskills hotel with a quintet for forty dollars a week—forty dollars for the quintet, that is—sleeping bunkhouse-style in a chicken shack across the road: "We couldn't go home," the celebrated composer remembered. "The city meant polio in those days. We were like prisoners. One morning we woke up to fire engines. The hotel had burned down. We cheered." Surprise mounted and then reassurance prevailed as Bacharach's Penelope was discovered to be the actress Angie Dickinson. Dickinson had been known and loved by the public when Bacharach was little more than Mr. Dickinson, when "Magic Moments" had been a Perry Como recording and Gene Pitney was singing "The Man Who Shot Liberty Valence" with never a thought for the man who had written "The Man Who Shot...."

Finally, his public thrilled to the revelation that Bacharach had been an arranger and accompanist for entertainers of equal or higher fame: Vic Damone, the Ames Brothers, Steve Lawrence, and most important Marlene Dietrich. Dietrich of course was no mere entertainer. More than a hero, she was a goddess, and Bacharach's intimacies with her constituted an important part of his legend. Like Odysseus before him, whose mythic sponsor was Athene, Bacharach had been touched by Olympians. "She's the most generous and giving woman I know," he once said of Dietrich. "If I had a cold she'd swamp me with vitamin C. She once pulverized six steaks for their juice to give me energy. She used to wash my shirts." Could Odysseus have said as much? And serving as a talisman of his Olympian connections was a Dior plaid mohair scarf some twelve feet long given to him by Dietrich while he accompanied her on the international concert stage:

> When I arrived in Poland to meet Marlene, she was waiting for me, in a snowstorm, at the airport with this scarf, so I'd be warm.... I can't wear bizarre clothes [he added, attesting to the acceptance of the talisman], but anything Marlene gave me always felt sensible and right.

To Bacharach's popular homage and formal recognition, to the development of his hero's image and legend, there was in the 1970s the beginning of *commemoration,* particularly in the formation of Bacharach fan clubs. And what of the sociologist's final criterion, *cult establishment?* Surely that would have required a fiery death by airplane (a la Will Rogers or Buddy Holly) or automobile (James Dean), or an assassination (Lincoln or Lennon), or a mystery eternally unresolved (Amelia Earhart). After a respectful period of mourning, of course, a commemorative stamp could be issued, though Bacharach presumably prefers mortal life to immortal heroism. And in any case by the mid-1970s he had fulfilled most of the processes with which hero-watchers are familiar.

But if his passage through this hero-making sequence had observers of American popular culture standing at attention, so did Bacharach's uncanny adherence to another cluster of sociological criteria, the rules for the creation of popular heroes. We defer once again to the sociologist Klapp:[4]

Hero-making situations. Heroes like bacteria live best in congenial environments. For the hero the Petri dish may be a grand political or military crisis, some stupendous scientific or artistic achievement, a mere theatrical or sporting event. Indeed any situation is potentially hero-making if it focuses public attention on some unmet need. Burt Bacharach's was such an environment, for the world of popular music is always in the public eye. Americans annually spend more than a billion dollars on recorded popular music. The demand for popular tunes is insatiable, the locale everywhere. Moreover in music, as in most things, Americans have what the historian and culture watcher Daniel Boorstin has called "extravagant expectations."[5] The music must not only keep coming, it must be original and stimulating. The latest tune must also be the greatest tune. Hence the composer or musician—and Bacharach was both—becomes Sisyphus in a spotlight, forever rolling his stone through the glare of public attention toward an unmet need.

Heroic role. The situation established, the hero must rise to the occasion by fulfilling one or another of the many heroic roles that the culture makes available. Could Bacharach have become the conquering hero (a la Beowulf or Babe Ruth) or the clever hero (Br'er Rabbit) whose brains triumph over brawn? Or could he have become the avenging hero (James Bond), the benefactor (Robin Hood), or the martyr (Joan of Arc)? In the mold of American heroes past, Bacharach was none of these so much as he was a Cinderella. His image cut, as has been noticed, in an Algeresque style, Bacharach was the "dark horse" who came in first: obscure but worthy origins, "instant" success in his late thirties after decades of hard work and soft returns. Even in success he remained the Cinderella man surmounting adversity: legend has it that when *Promises, Promises* was in Boston preparing for Broadway it was decided that another song would be needed. Lyricist Hal David and Bacharach—the latter haggard from a bout of pneumonia that had put him into the hospital—wrote the song in a single day. It entered the show immediately. Sick men do not write songs in a single day of course; heroes in turn write hits: the tune, "I'll Never Fall in Love Again," was subsequently recorded by Dionne Warwick and spent several weeks on the record charts.*

---

*Curiosity regarding "hardship" as a precondition of success in America led the sociologist Leo Lowenthal through a content analysis of 168 popular biographies. He discovered that "troubles and difficulties with

Color. "The quality of 'color'," says Klapp, "seems to be in actions or traits which excite popular interest and imagination." *Color* if you will is a paler shade of charisma. *Color* is Muhammad Ali's circling style of pugilism and doggeral style of poetry. *Color* is the way that Jack Kennedy said "viga," and the way that his brother Bobby nervously fought his tousled locks and the way every Kennedy played touch football. *Color* also invests the properties of heroes: Roosevelt's cigarette holder and Churchill's cigar, King Arthur's Excalibur and Patton's pearl-handled pistols, Christ's seamless robe and the comic-strip character Linus' filthy blanket.

For Bacharach of course *color* was in part his image and legend, his handsome features and his clothing, his flamboyant style of musical conducting, the stories which came to surround him. His most precious and *colorful* possession though was his music. Complex and sophisticated, Bacharach songs cannot be aimlessly whistled by the man on the street. Indeed many professional entertainers have found them difficult to perform.* Most popular music is written to formula—4/4 or occasionally 3/4 time, four 8-bar phrases finishing a 32-bar song—a fact which explains the popular composer's ability to meet the insatiable demands of the listening public. In Bacharach's music however the formulae of regular rhythms are absent. One passage of the song "Promises, Promises," for example,

which the road to success is paved" are so commonplace that they "are discussed in the form of stereotypes." Over and over again we hear that the going is rough and hard.... Defeat or stalemate [are reported] in matter-of-fact tone, rather than [as] descriptions of life processes." In William Peterson, ed., *American Social Patterns* (Garden City, 1956), pp. 93-94.

*Dionne Warwick: "You've practically got to be a music major to sing Bacharach." Polly Bergen: "I did 'A House is Not a Home recently—a great song. But I never did get the timing. I made them write it so I could end up with the band—regardless of how I got lost along the way, and did I ever."

moves from 3/4 time to 4/4, 3/4, 5/4, 3/4, 4/4, 6/4, 3/4, 4/4, 6/4, 3/4, 3/8, 4/8, 4/4, 5/4 and back to 3/4 time. For toe-tappers the results are discouraging; for more careful listeners they are exciting and unpredictable. Nor does Bacharach's music suffer the 8-to-the-bar syndrome. Some songs—"Are You There (With Another Girl)?" comes to mind—are written in orthodox but unconventional 6-bar phrases. Others, such as "the Look of Love" and "I Say a Little Prayer," pretend orthodoxy only to be punctuated by the rambunctious urgency of an occasional measure in 2/4 time. Still other pieces are written with formal rhythms, but only it would seem to keep the band together; the phrases, musical and lyrical, have patterns and pulses of their own. Listen for instance to "A House is Not a Home," "The Windows of the World," or "Make it Easy on Yourself." Phrasing dictates rhythm, not vice versa as in formula tunes.* And as music critic Charles Champlin pointed out: "He has a way of doing unconventional things [not only] with time, with the length of a phrase, [but also] with chord patterns and the logic by which one note follows another." There is in short a Bacharachian flavor to Bacharach's music, a distinctive spirit that without making them all sound alike stamps each of his songs with his marque. And in the marque there is *color*. To ponder him without his music was to see him in two dimensions: the graying temples and the soft voice and the Dietrich scarf may be there, but watching him performing his music was seeing him literally in living *color*.

Personal Traits. Klapp has written that the personal habits and characteristics of heroes are relatively unimportant to their heroism. "Distance," said the sociologist, "builds the 'great man'," distance that stands as a buffer between the intimacies of the hero and the curiosities of the clamoring millions. Still any personal

---

*These examples are conveniently available on either *Burt Bacharach: Reach Out* (A&M 131) or *Burt Bacharach: Make it Easy on Yourself* (A & M SP4188).

traits that may reach an attentive public might augment greatness, especially if those traits are consistent with the hero's role or the hero's *color*. So Babe Ruth whose heroism grew from his prowess as a batter was the more awesome after scientists declared his hand/eye coordination to be superior to that of most other humans. So also Bacharach. A tireless professional consumed by his music, each of Bacharach's television concerts included a glimpse of his working day: the creation, movieola at his side, of a motion picture score, or the production, Dionne Warwick at his side, of another hit record. Each program displayed him as a perfectionist who drove his musicians with the intensity of a plantation overseer, only to be doted on in spite of it.

But in Bacharach the public saw more than a man dedicated to his music, the admitted root and base of his fame. In his home they saw themselves writ large: his wife Angie Dickinson and their daughter Lea Nikki, born in 1967, were everyman's family, though made of finer stuff. And the family Bacharach lived in a luxurious home in Beverly Hills. Luxurious but rented, and what could have been more fitting: it may be well for ancient heroes to have resided in temples of stone, so static was their world. But in the realm of popular music, a frenetic and whirling scene, action is the essence. Thus for Bacharach the sumptuous but rented temple was appropriate. "I'm an impatient man," he allegedly said. "I go one month at a time. That's why Angie and I rent the house. I couldn't wait for one to get built."

And then it ended. By the close of the decade the "Music Man 1970" was a has-been. His marriage to Dickinson had ended in divorce. One of Tinpan Alley's more popular and profitable relationships—the collaboration of composer Bacharach, lyricist David, and songstress Warwick—had terminated in courtroom acrimony with Warwick suing her erstwhile compatriots for $5.5 million and subsequently winning an out-of-court settlement. In 1973 his and the film producer Ross Hunter's much publicized extravaganza, a musical version of the Shangra La fable *The Lost Horizon* that had been made so famous in print by James Hilton and on the screen by Frank Capra, failed as massively at the box office as *Butch Cassidy and the Sundance Kid* had succeeded. "A big stale marshmellow," it was called by the *New York Times* critic Vincent Canby.* By 1981 the weekly celebrity magazine *People* had Bacharach "seeking to rebound from some lean professional years," a search that is hardly the stuff of heroes.

So the man who even by sociological standards seemed to be a hero turned out instead to be a mere celebrity, a man who, as Boorstin has written, "is known for his well-knownness." It was easy for us to be fooled as we watched him maneuver the gauntlet: popular homage turned to formal recognition, and image and legend were constructed and commemorated if not cultified. So too the hero-making situation and the heroic role, *color* and compatible personal traits: all were in place.

Still there is a crucial distinction between celebrity and hero. Popular celebrities it turns out are not classical heroes. Peanuts is not Achilles. Greta Garbo, though in her time a celebrity of brilliant radiance, was but an eyeblink as compared to the history of the Odysseus cult. Perhaps the distinction is best caught in Bacharach's rented mansion in Beverly Hills. Perhaps like his house Bacharach was a rented hero. For like Bacharach the millions who celebrate celebrities are themselves impatient people who "go one month at a time." They too live in a popping, whirling scene, and whoever would be smitten by their worship must be a moving target. Until yesterday humankind lived in an arrested and static world. To be heroic in the eyes of the ancients was to personify the values of an arrested culture. But the pace of change has accelerated. To be an ancient hero—to *stand* for something—is in our electronic universe to be obsolete. These days one must *move* for something, and

*Canby did opine in passing that Bacharach's "music...is often pleasant, but it's too sophisticated for...the movie."

Bacharach in his own season moved mightily. The rise and fall of Burt Bacharach is a study in motion, a reflection of the frenetic nature of his—and our—times. Bacharach, thought a hero, was a mere celebrity. But he doubtless wonders, do you know how hard it is to become a celebrity?

Three

Gasoline Station:
The Evolution of a Vernacular Form

In their book *American Skyline* the urbanists Christopher Tunnard and Henry Hope Reed argued that the form of a people's architecture is a clue to a people's character. Thus it was fitting they said that the skyline of seventeenth-century Boston should be dominated by church spires even as twentieth-century New York is a forest of commercial towers. What literally more concrete way to symbolize the evolution of a nation's ethos from religion to business?[1] The thesis, though sensible enough, has not been adopted by many historians of American architecture, however. For if it be fair, the proper study of modern, industrialized, and mobile American society should examine not only the stately skyscraper but also the lowly filling station. After all, in the United States 150 million motor cars annually consume 120 billion gallons of gasoline purchased at one or another of the 200,000 service stations that punctuate the landscape. The stations themselves are then symbolic of America's contemporary, motorized society, for in a very literal sense they pump the lifeblood of its mobile culture. Little wonder then that service stations should be celebrated in pop art by the painter Edward Ruscha and others. Little wonder also that a major American petroleum company should include in its promotional material the thesis: "service stations are uniquely essential to our modern way of life." And little wonder finally that the service station—at first glance a mere shell whose function is its sole significance—should have developed an important and instructive though largely ignored architectural form.

Scrutinize if you will the service stations that since the 1930s have been designed and built by the Marathon Oil Company. Marathon is a major American retailer of petroleum products, ranking near the top one hundred largest industrial corporations in the United States. Between 3,500 and 4,000 of its service stations are located in the mid-western and southern states, and each is typical of the architecture found throughout the industry and across the continent. They are a convenient sample of the whole. But what does the sample say about the whole? And what does the whole say about the culture?

The Marathon Oil Company—or more precisely its corporate predecessors—developed three standardized service station types between its entry into the market place in 1933 and the close of World War Two. The smallest, descriptively called the "Metal Portable Service Station," was a metal-and-glass shell with porcelain enamel interior and concrete floor. Some twelve by eighteen feet, it contained a waiting room, rest rooms and a small storage area. But the "Metal Portable Service Station," the company's first effort at standardized architectural design, was a failure: conceived for prefabrication on a mass scale, fewer than a half-dozen were actually constructed; portable and therefore able to follow the changing patterns of the market, none was ever moved; euphemistically called a *service* station, it was really little more than a *filling* station, the pumping of fuel being its only function. For all of these reasons—the last being first, given the demand for general automotive servicing as well as simple refueling—"Metal Portable Service Station" died, leaving as survivors two remaining pre-war designs with less descriptive names: "Standard Service Station No. 2" and "Standard Service Station No. 3." A shadow of the first type remained however, for both "No. 2" and "No. 3" consisted of, first, a customer area containing a waiting room, restroom, and a storage room, and second, one or more service areas—or sheds for lubrication, washing, and other maintenance activities—appended to

Marathon Pre-War Station "Metal Portable Service Station"
Courtesy Marathon Oil Company

Marathon Pre-War Station, "Standard Service Station, No. 2,"
Courtesy Marathon Oil Company

Marathon Pre-War Station, "Standard Service Station No. 3,"
Courtesy Marathon Oil Company

the customer module. The former of course was a vestige of "Metal Portable Service Station," in "No. 2" a hexagonal structure and in "No. 3" an indented rectangle. In both cases the service areas were rectangular structures some twelve or fourteen by twenty-four feet.[2]

Though none of these early designs survived World War Two each of them was a prototype of all the service stations that would subsequently be constructed. And little wonder, for each of them precisely embodied the characteristics that the scholar John Kouwenhoven a few years later would call the "vernacular tradition." Indeed one cannot view these buildings without immediately recognizing the essence of the tradition: "economy, simplicity and flexibilty."[3] What better way to describe either these early structures or, as it turned out, those that would follow?

Economy. Each of the types had been conceived with inexpensive replication as the goal. Perhaps a hundred or more individuals of each type could therefore be built with no major alteration of design. Moreover all of the types were designed for easy and inexpensive maintenance. Concrete floors, metal and subsequently concrete block walls, porcelain enamel interiors—a material that would come to dominate a generation of vernacular architecture: these were the components of the Marathon service stations.

Simplicity. "Economy of line, lightness, strength, and freedom from meaningless ornament"—words that Kouwenhoven used in describing Donald McKay's nineteenth-century clipper ships—are a shorthand as well for the twentieth-century service station. Only the garish two-story hexagon of "Standard Service Station No. 2" stands as an exception to the rule.*

Flexibility. Each of the types was an invention in the

---

*Marathon Oil Company had two corporate predecessors, the Lincoln Oil Company whose motif was a lighthouse and the Ohio Oil Company which was particularly taken by the hexagon. "No. 2's" elaborate service module was the homely child of this marriage.

broadest sense, an architectural contrivance that could be located wherever a retail petroleum outlet was needed. Most important each was conceived to be a series of modules—basic structural elements—which could be horizontally stacked to produce a multiplicity of service station types with only a small repertoire of modules. As has already been shown, a given module—*bay* is the industry's term—could be designed to function as a customer or a service area. In subsequent years modules would be designed as storage rooms, vending areas, small restaurants, and the like. Bays would be mixed and matched, stacked high and stacked low (that is many modules or few), depending upon the class or size of station desired. In brief the service station was becoming a variation on Eli Whitney's theme of interchangeable parts.

If vernacular was the flavor of Marathan Oil Company's pre-war stations the tradition was only heightened in the so-called "porcelain box" architecture that typified the post-war decades. For Marathon it began with "4 bay standard," an expansive structure that the company built on a limited scale between 1947 and 1949. A nation relieved by the armistice—with its corresponding termination of fuel rationing—and looking forward to the prosperity of the post-war decade could scarcely find a more fitting symbol than "4 Bay Standard." Filling station, service center and store combined, it consisted of four rectangular modules, each fourteen by twenty-eight feet, standing in an I configuration. In keeping with the evolution that had begun before the war "4 Bay Standard" emphasized both sales and service with a pair of bays devoted to each and the latter pair partitioned into a foyer, waiting room, sales area, office and rest rooms. Interior appointments included brick floors and walls of ceramic tile; exteriors were of glass and of course porcelain enamel. Something of an extravagance, in size alone "4 Bay Standard" was two or three times larger than "Standard Service Station No. 3."

"Porcelain boxes" of a less elaborate nature followed,

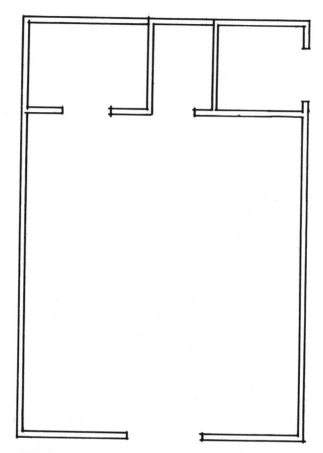

Marathon Station Floorplans, "Metal Portable Service Station," Courtesy Marathon Oil Company

and the genre, though now itself obsolete, became the most familiar form of service station architecture. Not for nothing, for instance, was it the "porcelain box" that Ruscha captured in his *Standard Service Station, Amarillo, Texas.* Marathon built more than 600 such stations between 1948 and 1969, many of which are still in use. First among them was "3 Bay Standard," of which nearly 400 individuals were constructed. Each was an I of three modules of fourteen by twenty-eight feet, two of which were designed for service.

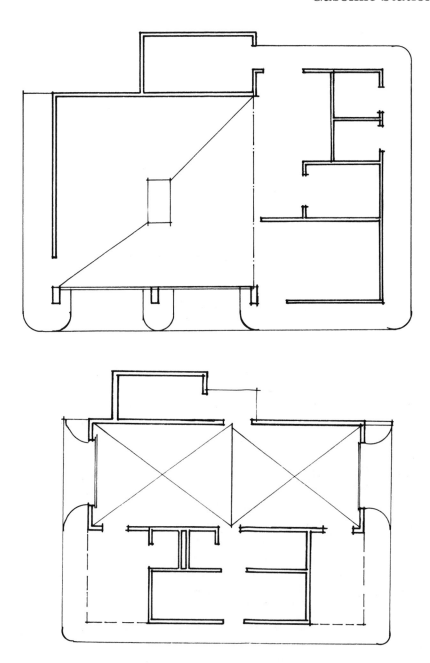

Marathon Station Floorplans, upper, "3 Bay Standard Modified," lower, "R.B." Courtesy Marathon
Oil Company

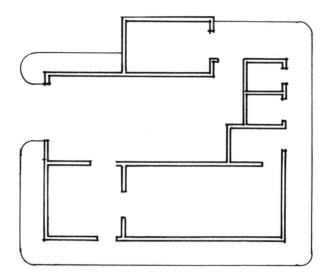

Marathon Station Floorplan, "FV,"
Courtesy Marathon Oil Company

the third for sales. Outside porcelain enamel pilasters separated the modules from each other and supported a simple roofline slab. Alterations of a cosmetic or modestly functional nature followed: "SM" (for "Standard Modified") enjoyed deeper service modules and deeper pilasters, as well as an additional minor module at the rear of the structure; "FM" ("Facade Modified") added the crown-shaped self-illuminated roofline that was so characteristic of American popular architecture in the 1950s and 60s; and "FB" ("Facade Brow") extended the crown roofline of "FM" along either side of the building.

Meanwhile at least two other "porcelain boxes" evolved beyond cosmetics to test the true flexibility of the vernacular tradition. During the 1960s Marathon built fifty-one of its type "RB" ("Rear Bay"). Though cosmetically similar to both "FM" and "FB," the rear-bay model departed from the usual I configuration and aligned its modules instead in a V shape. Placing the modules lengthwise, with service bays—

often the scene of noise and grime—to the rear of the sales bay, designers were able to give the station a more pleasing image. Minor changes also ensued: the modules grew slightly in size and small patios were appended to the sales bay. But the typical "porcelain box" motif was retained, hiding an imaginatively altered configuration of structural modules. Another interesting example of flexibility through interchangeability was the "FV" ("Facade Vending"). In "FV" as in "RB" the unsightly service area—now reduced to a single bay—was relegated to the rear of the building. The front in turn was given over to a sales area and to a larger room that could function as a vending area, store, or even a small restaurant. Outside little had changed: porcelain enamel pilasters rose to support a crown-facade roofline. Inside, however, as in "RB," the modules had been configured in a new way.

The Marathon Oil Company built the last of its "porcelain boxes" in 1969. Other structures of the genre continued to be built of course, not only by oil companies as service stations but in metamorphosed form as hot dog stands, pizzerias, doughnut shops, car washes and we shall eventually see, as fast-food eateries. Indeed to perceive of the American roadside without the "porcelain box" is a sobering task. All of which is only logical of course, for "porcelain-box" architecture is merely the reaction of the vernacular tradition to an expanding mobility. It is the soul of economy and simplicity and flexibility, the architectural extension of Whitney's interchangeable parts. "Form follows function" was the architect Louis Sullivan's caveat, but the minions of anonymous gas station draftsmen took him more literally than he ever cared to take himself.

In the 1970s however various forces conspired to replace the "porcelain box" with newer and more aesthetically pleasing architectural forms. In part these forces were political: municipalities became determined that service stations and the like would harmonize with the neighborhoods that they serve. In part too they were economic, as oil retailers in the attempt to stay abreast with

Marathon "Porcelain Box Stations," 4 Bay Standard,"

Marathon Porcelain Box Stations, "FM,"
Courtesy Marathon Oil Company

Marathon Porcelain Box Station, "RB,"
Courtesy Marathon Oil Company

Marathon "Porcelain Box" Stations, "FV,"
Courtesy Marathon Oil Company

or ahead of each other made stylistic changes which, taken en masse, constituted an industry-wide epidemic of architectural innovation. With few exceptions, then, by the end of the 1970s oil companies were constructing what they called "design" stations, structures consistent with both the demands of local government and the dictates of the marketplace.

Marathon for its part has created four "design" types. "Colonial," a style that actually made its debut in 1962 and went into full production in the late 1960s, takes its name from its ruling motif. A brick veneer exterior, columns and pilasters, hipped and gabled roof, cupola and weathervane: all are contrived to lend an eighteenth-century aura to an intrinsically twentieth-century-structure. "Alpine" like "Colonial" takes its name from its decor. The A-frame roofline, glass-and-wood exterior, and wood-paneled interior—as well, one might add, as its geographic location, for virtually all of the "Alpine" individuals are located in Michigan—all join to produce a recognizable image. "R-75" (or "Route 75") draws its name from the interstate thoroughfare that links the midwest—Marathon's major market—with Florida. Located along the route, "R-75" is a brick-and-glass structure with substantial sales and vending areas and a relatively small service area. The configuration is sensible given the interstate traveler's greater need for fuel and snacks than for lubrication or repairs. And most important if only in numbers is "Kettering," so named because the city of Kettering, Ohio, was the site of the prototype. First built in 1967, "Kettering" quickly became the company's most popular "design" station. Bay front and cathedral ceiling on the sales area, and crown facade roofline over the service areas—the latter remininiscent of the "porcelain box": these are "Kettering's" distinctive features.

Since its inception each of these types has nicely fulfilled the demands that have been placed upon the entire "design" generation of service stations. Each has been aesthetically pleasing particularly when contrasted to its

Marathon Design Station, "Colonial,"
Courtesy Marathon Oil Company

Marathon Design Station, "Alpine,"
Courtesy Marathon Oil Company

Marathon Design Station, "Kettering,"
Courtesy Marathon Oil Company

Marathon "Design" Stations, "Kettering"
Courtesy Marathon Oil Company

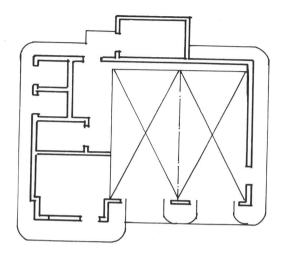

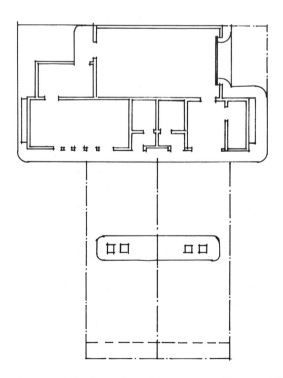

Marathon Station Floorplans, upper, "Colonial,"
lower "R-75." Courtesy Marathon Oil Company

"porcelain box" ancestors, and each therefore has met the specifications of municipal governments as well as the requirements of the marketplace. If in aesthetic terms much is new in structural terms little has been changed. Compare for instance the floor plans of "Colonial" and the older "SM." In the "design" station the sales module is extended slightly—an accommodation to the motif's pilasters-and-columns treatment—but "Colonial" and "SM" otherwise share an identical configuration. In a single I file stand a sales module—partitioned into waiting room, office/storage area—and rest rooms, and two or more service bays of equally familiar description. "Colonial" in short is really "SM" in eighteenth-century costume. Indeed Marathon has often celebrated the blood line by renovating its "porcelain boxes" through the application of colonial motifs. So skillful is the renovation—but more to the point of course so structurally oldstyle is the genuine "Colonial"— that the untrained eye seldom detects the "porcelain box" behind the "design."

Similarly "R-75" resembles the older "FV." Both types emphasize sales over service; consequently both relegate a single service bay to the rear of the structure, freeing the facade for sales and vending functions. And finally there is "Kettering."* At first glance the floor-plan appears to depart from the modular scheme of things, though here too the pattern prevails. In creating "Kettering" designers say that they simply began with the "SM," its service bay rotated ninety degrees. Finding it too small they enlarged the sales area by bulging the front wall into a figurative as well as literal bay window. The placement of doors on the sales areas was usually altered to provide for a side entry, thereby hiding the noise and grime of automotive maintenance behind an attractive wall of bricks which rises from a hedge of ornamental shrubbery.

Thus Marathon's "design" stations are intriguing not

---

*"Alpine," built on "Kettering's" floorplan, can be safely ignored.

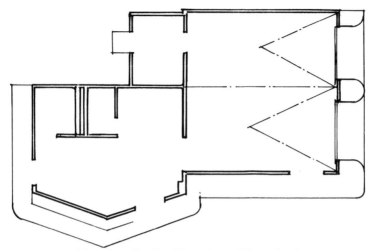

Marathon Station Floorplans, "Kettering"
Courtesy Marathon Oil Company

only because they are examples of the entire industry's response to the repeal of the "porcelain box," but more important because they illustrate the durability of the vernacular tradition in American architecture. They illustrate, that is, the enduring utility of modular design, whether the costume be portable metal or colonial cupola. Here in these "design" types, no less than before, a small repertoire of modules can be stacked in a variety of configurations to produce a variety of individual stations. The concept of modularity, seen first in its survival from type to type within a generation and second in its survival from generation *to* generation, is as easily illustrated by the variety of configurations available within a single type. "Kettering" for instance, true to the dictates of the vernacular tradition, is so flexible that its modules can be stacked in an immense variety of ways. Thus one station becomes another as the modules are shuffled. Larger stations are built by the mere addition of service bays. And compatible configurations can be combined to give, for instance, a sales module flanked on one side by a pair of service bays and on the other by a small restaurant or grocery store. Nor, it need hardly be said, is this unique to

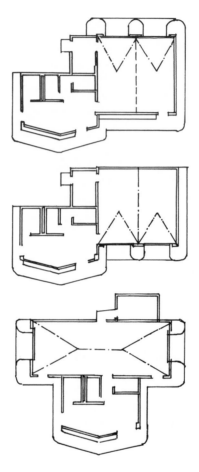

The configurations of Marathon's "Kettering,"
Courtesy of Marathon Oil Company

"Kettering"; similar configurations can be drawn from virtually every station ever built by Marathon Oil Company, endlessly proving the flexibility of the vernacular.

The vernacular tradition is by definition seldom aesthetically pure, by intention rarely unique, and by scholarly custom usually beneath the level of cultural scrutiny. Yet as with advertising or celebrities, and as we shall see with other elements of commonplace American life, vernacular architecture is all around us in the form of franchised eateries, tract houses, and, yes, service stations. As do other examples of the tradition the service station speaks instructively of its intrinsic economy, simplicity and flexibility. And yet the lessons as always are not merely architectural but social and historical. The service station in this higher sense is an index of its culture. The service station's evolution and growth—from naive but hopeful "Metal Portable Service Station" to the imperious post-war "4 Bay Standard" and on to the latest "design" creation—is a lecture on the growth of mechanization and mobility. And finally its enduring modularity discloses the fact that in industrial cultures roadside shrines, like everything else, consist of interchangeable parts.

Four

Hamburger Stand: Industrialization and the Fast-Food Phenomenon

I n 1936 Charlie Chaplin unveiled one of the most famous of his satirical commentaries on life in the twentieth century. *Modern Times,* he called it—the film and the century—and his protagonist was a factory worker who stood at his station on the assembly line tightening a perpetual sequence of bolts, each with a single turn of a single wrench. Monotonously he thereby became an accessory to the replication of some standardized product or other. The motion picture was not named "best of the year"(an honor that went instead to a completely forgettable M.G.M. biography of *The Great Ziegfeld).* Its setting did have a certain recognizable madness, however, which doubtless explains why Chaplin's imagery has since become a cultural symbol.

Not that the helpless pawn of standardized industrial forces was a Chaplinesque invention. Historians among the audience of *Modern Times* knew its protagonist well. Long before him the handloom weavers of England had bowed before the power looms of the eighteenth century even as their fellows in a myriad of other callings had sooner or later fallen beneath some similar juggernaut. The conditions that Chaplin attacked with pathos and satire had in all seriousness and with great violence been confronted a hundred years earlier by the Luddites. Indeed so compelling

61

and ubiquitous had been the narrative that Chaplin's themes were major leitmotifs in the history of the industrial revolution: the subordination of the skilled artisan to the sophisticated mechanism, and the replacement of the unique item by the standardized product.

The times have changed now and, outside the Third World at least, civilization has moved through secondary and tertiary revolutions into what is often characterized as a post-industrial condition. And yet the dichotomies of artisan versus mechanism and unique versus standard—couplets so central to the revolution of the nineteenth century—still exist here and there in post-industrial settings. Indeed one such place is suggested by *Modern Times* itself: as aficionados will recall, Chaplin had his masochistic protagonist actually suggest that the purposes of the factory might be further served by a feeding machine that would oblige the laborers to eat without loss through down time. The suggestion was thought too complicated by management, but the most cursory glance at the American landscape of the 1970s and 1980s suggests that it need not have been. Franchised eateries stand cheek by jowl along every post-industrial city's neon strip. A handful of nationally recognized trade names—each itself a near icon—with thousands of individual eateries snuggled beneath them gives evidence of both the mechanical feasibility and the manifold profitability of feeding machines. The industrial revolution in short has come to fast food, and it is well to examine its advent. In doing so we may recapture in our own time the processes by which industrialization occurs. Moreover we may learn something about the impact that industrialization and its imperatives have had on American culture, a culture that quite literally takes much of its sustenance in the form of the machine-made hamburger.

The pre-industrial history of the fast-food phenomenon in the United States disappears somewhere into the *diner* (an Americanism of nineteenth-century vintage). Originally a railroad car especially equipped for the preparation and serving of food, the diner came to be a derailed shell or an erstwhile trolley following its calling in a single location. Or perhaps a more recognizable form of pre-industrialization in fast food is the *greasy spoon* (a colloquialism with roots apparently as deep as the 1920s), that franchised or company-owned edifice of the post-war period, that Royal Castle or White Castle or White Tower or Toddle House that in many cases continues to punctuate the American cityscape. Take for instance any one of the many Royal Castle restaurants that between 1938 and 1975 were constructed and operated by the Miami-based firm Royal Castle System, Incorporated. Even in the worst of years Royal Castle made more than twenty millions of dollars in sales.[1] In terms both financial and symbolic then the local Royal Castle was a fitting archetype of pre-industrialism in fast food.

The sample might conform to any of the four types that the Royal Castle System constructed during its thirty-seven years in fast food: "D," the earliest of the four, was a rectangle thirty-five by forty feet, a forward corner recessed into a front entrance. Type "DD" followed, essentially a "D" structure augmented by a smaller module whose interior was fitted for table service. The "J" came next, a slightly smaller building—twenty-eight by forty feet—whose exterior featured the same illuminated facade that dominated gasoline service station architecture during the period. And finally came the "K" type, a square of thirty-five feet with an exaggerated hip roof. Only the "K" departed from tradition by obscuring its kitchen behind a partition, a service passage joining preparation and serving areas. The other types were vintage greasy spoon: delineating their interiors was the service counter; flanking the counter a row of stools and a galley-style kitchen.

Structures of such modest artistic pretensions have of course generally lain beneath the purview of scholarly scrutiny. A few architectural historians have stooped to comment however, some with disgust, others with glee, and

Royal Castle Restaurant, "D,"
Courtesy George Chillag

The Royal Castle, "DD,"
Courtesy George Chillag

Royal Castle, "J"
Courtesy George Chillag

Royal Castle, "K"
Courtesy George Chillag

all on the apparent divorce of image from function. The critic Reyner Banham for instance was clearly disturbed by such matters when he explained how one might construct a "hamburger bar" by purchasing "a plain standard building shell from Butler Buildings Corporation or a similar mass-producer and add[ing] symbolic garnish [or signs] to the front, top, and other places that show."[2] In contrast the architect Robert Venturi and his associates have applauded this genre of structure. Explaining how in many elitist "megastructures" the "systems of space, structure, and program [or function] are submerged and distorted by an overall symbolic form," in buildings such as a Royal Castle restaurant—the Venturi people call them "decorated sheds"—"systems of space and structure are directly at the service of program, and ornament is applied independently of them."[3]

One can then either denigrate with Banham the garnished shell and its inconsistencies of work and form, or celebrate with Venturi the decorated shed and its liberation of image from function. Either way it is worth noting that a Royal Castle restaurant, like a gasoline service station, is a good example of what John Kouwenhoven and others have called the "vernacular tradition." Each of the tradition's characteristics—"economy, simplicity, and flexibilty"—is on clear display.[4] Each of the Royal Castle types was designed for economical maintenance, with tile floors, concrete and glass walls, and either aluminum or the ubiquitous porcelain enamel fixtures. With the exception of the "K" and its excessive roof line, each is free of meaningless ornamentation. And each is an invention in the broadest sense of the term: an architectural contrivance that can be replicated over and over again without modification in design, and can be located wherever a fast-food eatery seems desirable. Indeed like their vernacular counterpart the service station, certain Royal Castle types—particularly the "D" and the "DD"—are so flexible that they are properly understood as a series of modules or basic structural elements that can be horizontally stacked to

produce a variety of restaurant types with a small repertoire
of module designs.

In the days before the industrial revolution enveloped
the fast-food business the door to a busy Royal Castle
restaurant was an entrance to an animated collage. Here a
derelict dozed in his coffee. Here a nurse fresh from a night's
sleep breakfasted on bacon and eggs while a cabbie weary
from a night on the streets relaxed over a hamburger. Here a
nondescript couple consumed any of the fifty-odd items that
appeared on the Royal Castle menu. The establishment in
short was a jostle of apparently disparate activities, each in
pursuit of its separate agenda.

Lending unity and coherence to this jostle however was
the presence of the protagonist, the artist-in-residence: the
fry cook (yet another colloquialism, this apparently of
unknown origin). As the protagonist he served as the
common denominator among these uncommon agendas
because he—and usually with single-handed dexterity—had
taken each order and had prepared and served its contents.
More important he was an artisan in the most classical
sense of the term: he had undergone an apprenticeship, he
was able to exercise special skills and manipulate special
equipment, he pursued an applied art. His education had
been of the most basic sort—on-the-job—so experience
rather than some more formal order of training accounted
for his expertise. His work bench so to speak was the galley
kitchen stretching from grill to ice maker, with coffee urns
and soup warmers, toasters and waffle irons, griddles and
sinks all strategically interspersed.

Scattered across the galley was an array of tools with
names as arcane and functions as specialized as those of the
tanner or the chandler. And finally his product—mean fare
to be sure—played soup and sandwich to the chef's souffle as
surely as the anonymous gargoyle played to Michelangelo's
Pieta, as surely as in more general terms the product of any
artisan plays to the more sophisticated but nevertheless
similar product of the artist. Was the handloom weaver the
protagonist of textile production before the introduction of

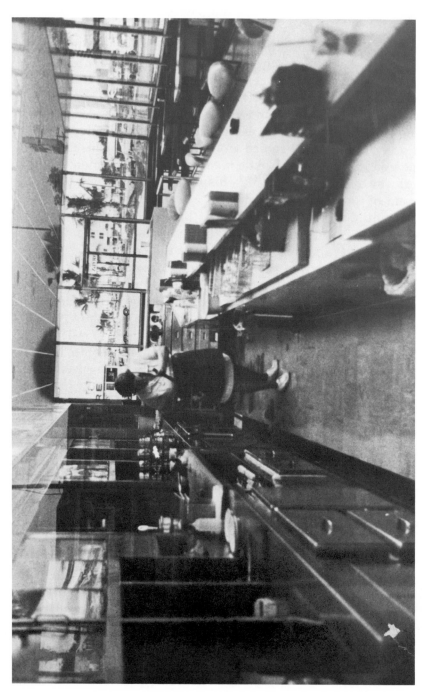

The Royal Castle Galley.
Courtesy George Chillag.

the power loom? Or the cooper the protagonist of barrel-making before the advent of the mass-produced steel drum? So as certainly the fry cook was the artisan-in-residence in this archetype of pre-industrial fast food, the greasy spoon.

In 1975 however after nearly four decades in the fast-food business, the Royal Castle restaurants and their artisans left the marketplace. Clearly they had become the victims of technological obsolescence, for down the road was new competition, a new variety of structures that housed a new central character and offered a new and standardized product. Industrialization had come to fast food.

The Burger King Corporation, a subsidiary of the Pillsbury Company was in 1980 operating or franchising 2,700 fast-food stores world-wide. Its sales were exceeding 1.8 billion dollars annually, making it one of the largest fast-food firms in America.* And each of its restaurants is the home of the industrialized hamburger.

Like its pre-industrial predecessor the Royal Castle System, the Burger King Corporation has constructed a variety of restaurant types during its decades of existence. In the 1950s the company relied upon the "Walk-up," a simple rectangle whose interior housed equipment for the preparation of food but lacked a seating area, rest-room facilities, and other amenities usually associated with American restaurant design. The "Handlebar" store followed. So named because of its dominant roofline decoration, the "Handlebar" was a rectangular structure, forty-five by fifty feet. In adherence to the flexibility of the vernacular tradition—and reminiscent of the Royal Castle's "D"-"DD" coupling—the "Handlebar" was merely a "Walk-Up" augmented by a seating area.

In recent years however Burger King stores have invariably conformed to either the "Red Roof" or "Natural Finish" types. Rectangular buildings of between forty-five

*Only MacDonalds Restaurants and the U.S. Army are larger.

Burger King, "Walk-Up"
Courtesy Burger King Corporation

Burger King, "Handlebar,"
Courtesy Burger King Corporation

Burger King, "Red Roof"
Courtesy Burger King Corporation

Burger King Restaurants, "National Finish"
Courtesy Burger King Corporation

by fifty feet and fifty by fifty-five feet depending upon the anticipated sales and desired seating capacity, these recent types are distinguishable from their predecessors as well as from each other by their distinctive decors. Gone is the earlier handlebar logo; in its place is either a red mansard roofline or an ecology motif: cedar shakes, brickwork walls and warm color schemes.

Too much can be made of these decors, of course, for the lessons of Banham and Venturi should always be borne in mind. Recalling the one's garnished shell and the other's decorated shed it quickly becomes clear that the Burger King Corporation has simply retired older for newer images. Moving one's attention from decoration to structure it becomes evident that the divorce of image from function which alternately appalled Banham and thrilled Venturi still prevails. Architecturally food preparation and seating areas lie side-by-side within rectangular boxes and the vernacular tradition is intact. Hence the eye is caught by that familiar economy of maintenance and simplicity of design. Noticed also is the flexibility and replicability of the structures. And finally, in the Burger King store as elsewhere within the tradition one finds the vernacular reliance upon a horizontal stacking of modules. Hiding behind a different logo then and clothed in a different wardrobe of motifs is the same vernacular tradition.

Inside the store however all is different. As our attention turns from architecture to cookery we cannot help but notice the conspicuous absence of the greasy spoon's protagonist and artisan-in-residence, the fry cook. Nor can we ignore his shining, stainless steel successor, a feeding machine that would have warmed Charlie Chaplin's satirical heart. Here between the fry cook and the feeding machine is the first of the industrial revolution's dichotomies: the artisan versus the mechanism. Not far behind is the revolution's second dichotomy: the unique versus the standard. For our new protagonist is the Burger King broiler and it is producing Burger King 'burgers by the thousand. Industrialization has come to fast food.

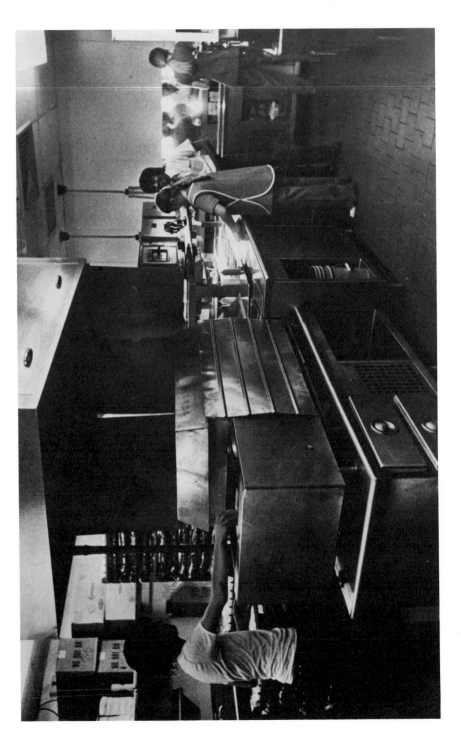

The Burger King Line-Up.
Courtesy George Chillag.

Like other machinery in the world of industrialization the Burger King Corporation's hamburger machine—or *line-up,* as it is referred to in the trade—rationalizes the construction of its product. Accordingly the process is first separated into its discreet tasks. Each task is then assigned to its proper station, mechanical or manual, a post that has been carefully designed for a precise purpose. And finally each of these stations is assigned its appropriate place along the assembly line. In the world of Burger King the line-up begins with a broiling mechanism. Moving along endless-grate conveyors, buns of bread and patties of ground meat travel at precise speeds through intense temperatures. When properly cooked these patties and buns leave the grates and descend small chutes, the one to be sandwiched within the other. These sandwiches are then moved to the next station, a preparation table where a variety of accessories and condiments is applied as prescribed by the customer.* Here the sandwich is completed, packaged and forwarded to the point of sale.

The Burger King line-up is of course no more sophisticated than its product necessitates. Still students of, say, Oliver Evans' eighteenth-century plant at Redclay Creek or Henry Ford's twentieth-century works at River Rouge will nevertheless recognize the line-up's mechanical essence. As the historian Siegfried Giedion has explained:

> Mechanizing production means dissecting work into its component operations...[and] in manufacturing complex products such as the automobile [or as we see relatively simple products such as the hamburger sandwich], this division goes together with re-assembly.[5]

When contrasted with the pre-industrial nature of the Royal Castle System's greasy spoon, the Burger King line-

---

*Hence the advertiser's jingle: "...special orders don't upset us, / all we ask is that you let us / have it your way."

up conjures an overtly industrial milieu. The basic elements of the factory have obviously been introduced to the fast-food phenomenon. Moreover, this introduction has brought with it two other inevitable changes. One, the advent of the feeding machine has introduced the possibility—some consumers would say the dulling certainty—of a standardized, recognized product. As one commentator has written: "Burger King...wants the food it serves in New York to be as identical as humanly possible to that served in New Mexico or New Orleans." But conformity of this magnitude is of course not *humanly* possible; only machinery can provide so standardized a product. Concomitantly the rise of the machine has meant the fall of the artisan. Standing in the place of the fry cook, his lengthy education, his careful skills, and his arcane galley, is the glistening metal line-up and its inexperienced attendants. The Burger King Corporation claims that a single hamburger machine represents an investment in excess of seventy thousand dollars. It also claims that the average restaurant employee is an unskilled teenager who will work for the prevailing minimum wage and last perhaps four months on the job. What other data could more graphically illustrate the replacement of the experienced artisan with the sophisticated machine and its callow caretakers. In fast food as elsewhere the truth of Giedion's title cannot be escaped: mechanization takes command!

But what can they mean, all of these busy Burger King stores, all of these derelict Royal Castle restaurants, and all of the thousands upon thousands of other fast-food eateries that under competing logos punctuate the American landscape? Neither architecture of artistic merit nor engines of awesome sophistication can be found here. What lessons then are there, that this apparent trivia should be contemplated?

First we can look to the architecture of fast food to find another ready example of the vernacular tradition in building. And though as aesthetes we may be put off by the vulgarity of the tradition we cannot as students of the culture ignore its ubiquity. Vernacular architecture is all around us. If it is not as we have earlier seen a gasoline service station for the refueling of our automobiles, it is a Burger King for the refueling of our stomachs or a tract house for the renewal of our bodies. Inspirational as we might find the architecture of a Wright, a Sullivan, or a Stone, it is the vernacular tradition in which we live our lives. And the economy, simplicity and flexibility is readily evident in the houses of fast food.

Second, we can look inside the fast-food phenomenon to find an ongoing example of what it has meant to make an industrial revolution. And for students of industrialization who live as we do in cultures long since industrialized such examples are as useful as they are rare. In comparing the greasy spoon with the industrial hamburger one finds those imperatives of mechanization that students from before Adam Smith to after Giedion have explained to us: one, the standardized, uniform product; and two—if we may return all the way back to the seat of Charlie Chaplin's malaise— the subordination of the skilled artisan to the sophisticated mechanism.

These are the lessons, technological and cultural, of the industrialized hamburger.

Five

Short Short Story:
The Morphology of the Modern Fable

*G*ood Housekeeping, as each of its millions of readers must know, is "the magazine America lives by." Born a subliterary organ in 1885 and expanded in the 1930s to include both fiction and household hints, it has in our own time become nothing less than a trade journal for the American homemaker, a continuing compendium of advice and instruction, to quote the late historian Frank Luther Mott, on "family life and children, medical matters, cookery and foods, fashions and decorating, appliances, budgeting, [and] diet."[1] Never were the subliterary origins of *Good Housekeeping* forsaken, of course, for even now the editors continue the regular publication of novelettes, short stories, and a genre particularly appropriate to consumer journalism: short short stories.

But what, the uninitiated might ask, is a short short story? The short short story is first of all brief. "A complete story on these two pages," the billing inevitably promises. Not marked by brevity alone, however, the short short story is also entertaining, familiar and didactic. It is as it were a modern variant of the fable, a genre so prevalent within the oral tradition. For like the *Fables of Aesop* before them, the fables of *Good Housekeeping* are meant to convey some moral or useful lesson to their readers, that having read them those readers might in some transcendent sense become good housekeepers. One ponders these fables,

81

perhaps a thousand or more of them over the decades perused in kitchens and dentists' offices across the land, and the obvious queries come to mind: what systems of morality are proffered by these little fables? And how would one determine what systems are proffered?

Significantly the answer to the second of these questions comes from folklorists and anthropologists, from such seminal minds as Vladimir Propp and Claude Levi-Strauss.[2] It was they after all who explained what homemakers have presumably known by intuition: whether by Aesop or *Good Housekeeping* fables are constructed rather than written, and the structure of the fable is the key to the fable. As a sample one might take the fifty-two short short stories that appeared in the pages of *Good Housekeeping* between 1965 and 1970. These stories had been contributed by nineteen different authors—or pseudonyms—many of them polished professional writers whose works have been widely published.* In the manner of Levi-Strauss one might place these fifty-two stories, as it were, behind each other. One might then read them not from upper-left to lower-right but rather from front to back, simultaneously perusing the progress of *all* the stories even as reading casually one would note the progress of a single story.

In time it would become clear that there *is* but a *single* story. And written in morphological terms the story is this:

"To Trust in Andy," by Hugh Cave is a useful and polished example. Like its fellow fables it is constructed in distinct modules—after the structuralists we may refer to them as *motifs* and *bundles*—which are strung together in a linear pattern. *Linear morphology*, it might be called, meaning simply that the modules are arranged sequentially.[4] The story opens with its bundle of introductions: Andy is the hero; Maria, though the reader

---

*Because his story, "To Trust in Andy," is republished here as a sample of the genre, one thinks in particular of the writer Hugh Cave.[3] Cave's work has appeared in more than sixty anthologies and schoolbooks and at the 1978 World Fantasy Convention his *Murgunstrumm and Ohters* won the award for Best Collection.

The Linear Structure of the Short Short Story

Structural Bundles	Functions	Functions in "To Trust in Andy"
1. Introduction Bundle 1.1 Introduction of Hero 1.2 Introduction of Villain 1.3 Introduction of Tertiary 1.4 Introduction of Tertiary Characters	. . . in which the hero, villain, and tertiary characters are identified	Andy Graham is introduced Maria is introduced Arthur and Grace Graham are introduced
2. Problem Bundle 2.1 Confrontation Motif	. . . in which the struggle between hero and villain is revealed	Andy's relationship with Maria jeopardizes his plans for college
2.2 Transformation Motif	. . . in which the villain is revealed to be heroic	Maria is revealed to be eligible for college
3. Resolution Bundle 3.1 Solution Motif	. . . in which the solution to the confrontation is discovered	Maria will attend one of "a dozen colleges . . . on full scholarship."
3.2 Denouement Motif	. . . in which it is announced that they will live happily ever after	"With that they knew his future was safe. In his own strong hands."

"I won't be late," their son Andy said. "Just going over to Maria's and then to Prof Newell's house." He disappeared into the back hall and they could hear him polishing his shoes, slapping the cloth rhythmically as he hummed the high school song.

Hands in pocket, he strolled back into the living room where they sat. "There's a good band on Channel 10 at nine o'clock," he offered, smiling fondly at them. "If you want to hear some smooth trombones, don't miss it. See you." The door closed behind him.

It took a moment, or seemed to, for the echo of his presence to fade from the room. Then Grace Graham bit her lip and said, "Arthur, I'm worried. I think you ought to talk to him."

Arthur Graham put aside the evening paper and studied his wife's face. Twenty-six years of marriage had taught him to read it well, and he saw concern in it now. "You think it's serious?"

"I don't know," she said.

"Have *you* talked to him?" he asked.

"Not in that way. He's eighteen, and if you remember what our other son was like at that age—"

"I remember." He felt himself smiling. "No explanations, no communication. But he seems to have survived it all, Grace. His grades are up and he's a big man on the campus."

"There wasn't any girl, dear," she reminded him. "No *one* girl who really mattered."

"And this girl of Andy's ... what makes you think she matters?"

"He's rushing her," she said. "Tonight is the fifth straight night."

"What's she like?" he wanted to know.

"I've never laid eyes on her."

"I mean what does he *say* she's like."

"He hasn't said anything."

"He did tell us about meeting her."

"Well, yes. But that was over a month ago."

Arthur frowned: it *had* been quite a while back. He had not paid much attention to Andy's tale that evening, he recalled. He'd been tired after a long and difficult board meeting. Andy had taken part in some music affair out of town, some competition for high school students—the sort of thing he'd always won. This time the boy had been beaten by a girl who—what were his words?—"didn't even own her own instrument, but had to play on an old, beat-up horn she borrowed."

The girl was a senior at Hillwood High and had gone to the competition by bus, all alone. Andy had told her that though he went to Lincoln he lived in Hillwood too, and offered to drive her home. At first she'd refused. Then, discovering that she'd have to wait nearly two hours for a bus, she'd accepted.

She lived in a part of town that Andy did not know well; near the railroad tracks, on a street of run-down small houses that seemed to squeak when you looked at them. And one indeed did squeak, he learned as he walked her to the door.

At the door she hesitated, then finally asked him in. Maria, he discovered, had four brothers and two sisters—all younger than she and all living with their mother in four crowded rooms. Her father had died the year before in a mill accident. Her mother worked in a cafe on the same street. The girl introduced him to her mother—a small, tired woman who had nothing to say—and thanked him for his kindness. That should have been the end of it.

But it wasn't. Less than a week later, Andy had gone back.

When he had gone over it in his mind, Arthur Graham looked at his wife and said quietly. "We ought to decide just what it is we're against. Are we worried because he is spending too much time with *one* girl, or because it happens to be *this* girl?"

"The girl herself doesn't enter into it." Grace said quickly. "Not at all."

"Good. Because if we're objecting on that basis, we haven't a leg to stand on. Andy is what we've brought him up to be, and I think we ought to be very proud of him."

"We've never had reason not to be," she said simply, "and we've no reason now. Just yesterday I ran into Mildred Cummings—you know her; she teaches at Hillwood High. She'd seen Andy with Maria and she said Maria was one of the nicest girls she'd ever taught. Smart, too." She tried to smile. "No, it isn't Maria I object to. It would be any girl, Arthur. Andy's just so terribly young to get ... to get involved."

"No question about that." Arthur's fingertips drummed the end table beside his chair. "He's never gone steady before, has he? With all the girls he's brought around—all the many—there's never been anyone special like this."

"No. And that's another thing. He always *has* brought them around. But he hasn't brought Maria to meet us."

"Have you suggested he bring her?"

"No-o. If I seem to encourage it—"

"You're right, of course. If we put pressure on him, he's going to think we object to the girl herself, because of her home, her family. We both know how he'll react to that."

"He'll fight for her," Grace said. "He'll fight for the *idea* of her."

"We'd be disappointed in him if he didn't. All his life we've taught him to despise snobbery." He smiled assuringly at his wife. "Well, nothing much can happen. I suppose. Not really. He'll be going off to college in September."

"The Perkins boy was going off to college *last* September," Grace reminded him.

They were silent. Then Arthur stood up, thrusting his hands in his pockets. "I'll do what I can. When he comes in, I'll talk to him. Not about the girl, but about the importance of college and how fortunate he is that we can afford to send him." He crossed the big, comfortably furnished room and halted in front of the television set. "Let's look at that program he told us about."

The program was just ending when they heard their son's car in the driveway. The front door opened and closed. "Mom," Andy called. "Dad, Got company."

Tall, smiling, wholly at ease and self-assured, their son came into the room. The girl at his side was lovely, with dark hair and dark, luminous eyes —eyes so full of happiness that Arthur glanced quickly at his wife and saw, only because he knew her so well, her darting look of concern.

"This is Maria," Andy said. "Remember I told you about her."

Grace and Arthur greeted her warmly, and she accepted their welcome with those marvelously bright eyes and a gracious nod of her head.

"Got some news," Andy said excitedly, and Arthur could practically hear Grace's heart skip a beat as Andy's face lit up with pride. "I told you we were going over to Prof Newell's? The head of the music department at State?"

"Yes," Arthur Graham said.

"Well, he says there are at least a dozen colleges that Maria can get into—on a full scholarship. And he's going to see to it that she does. Now, how about that?"

"College?" Grace said faintly.

"With her talent and marks, she *has* to go to college. I've been telling her for weeks. And now she really can."

"I never thought I'd be able to," the girl whispered. "I just never even dared to dream that it was possible. I wouldn't even let myself think about it. Even now—well, it's just too much to believe."

"She's been laughing and crying all the way home," Andy said. "You never saw anyone so happy in your whole life."

"How wonderful for you," Grace said, reaching out to pat Maria's trembling hand.

"Look—Maria has to tell her mother," Andy explained. "Wait up for me, huh?"

Then they were gone, leaving Grace and Arthur staring at each other in silent astonishment.

Andy was gone longer this time. In fact, it was nearly midnight, when they heard the car in the driveway again. but they were not alarmed. Even when he flung himself into his favorite chair and told them he had taken Maria out again after taking her home—out to a drive-in for hamburgers and shakes "to celebrate the big event"—they could smile in their feeling of security and laugh a little inside.

For as he sat there with them in the living room, in his usual slouch with his long legs outthrust and the backs of his hands propping up his chin, they were aware of the difference in him. The change was not yet complete, perhaps, but it was there.

When he said, "Boy, what an evening," he was still the eighteen-year-old they had worried about. But with a kind of solemnity they had never heard before, he could also say—and did—"Can you imagine a girl with talent like that and no one *doing* anything about it? No one trying to help her?"

With that they knew his future was safe. In his own strong hands.   THE END

must wait a moment for her precise name, is the villain; and Andy's parents Arthur and Grace Graham lend tertiary support. The problem bundle quickly follows with its motifs of confrontation (i.e., will Andy's relationship with Maria jeopardize his plans for a college education?) and of transformation of villainy into heroism (no, for Maria is herself college-bound). Cave closes his fable with its resolution bundle, signing off by didactically paraphrasing they-lived-happily-ever-after with his own denouement motif: "With that they knew his future was safe. Safe in his own strong hands."

Variations of course exist. An occasional story alters the initial bundle by introducing the villain prior to the hero or by deleting the tertiary characters. More important there are two major variations. One of these can be called the *schizoid variant* in which heroism, villainy and therefore confrontation all exist within a single individual. In a typical example the housewife (hero) nostalgically confronts her premarital status as a career girl (villain) until some tertiary character (a thoughtful husband, say, or an injured child or a lonely spinster) recalls to her attention the intrinsic merits of housewifery. The second major variation might be called the *vanishing-villainy variant,* for here the villain is neither transformed (as in the basic structure) nor destroyed (as is usually the case in oral tradition) but simply disappears from the scene. A good example is the story of "Double Wedding," another Hugh Cave contribution. In "Double Wedding" two stereotypical sisters, a plain Jane (hero) and a prima donna (villain) marry their respective grooms in a double ceremony. During the reception which follows however the prima donna simply disappears, leaving plain Jane and her heroic values an unpretentious victory. But these variations whether minor or major do little to disturb the linearity of fables by *Good Housekeeping.* Introduction bundles are repetitiously succeeded by confrontation motifs and transformation (or vanishing-villainy) motifs, which are in turn repetitiously succeeded by solution motifs and denouement clauses.

There is however a second, though not contradictory, morphological pattern to these little fables, one which we might after Levi-Strauss call *binary morphology.*[5] To illustrate the binary essence of the short short story it will be useful to return to those stereotypical sisters in "Double Wedding." The plain Jane and the prima donna were actually the Nickerson sisters Mary and Beverly. And if the names are unfamiliar the personas are immediately recognizable. For instance.

> Not that the girl [Mary] was an ugly duckling, mind you. She wasn't anything like that, and was such a sweet child that most people wouldn't have noticed anyway. It was just that her sister Beverly was such an outright beauty that she became the main attraction at *any* affair, and Mary was bound to be second fiddle.

Or:

> Nobody paid much attention to her part of the wedding. Her sister Beverly was the prettiest bride you could ever hope to see, and marrying a mighty handsome fellow in

the bargain, and, to be blunt about it, people were scarcely aware that Mary and her freckled Will Prentice were there in the church at all.[6]

Similarly in "To Trust in Andy" one finds the hero disappearing "into the back hall and they could hear him polishing his shoes, slapping the cloth rhythmically as he hummed the high school song." Andy's older brother is a college student and "a big man on campus," while their father is an important executive who on the evening that he meets Maria is "tired after a long and difficult board meeting." Maria by contrast:

> lived in a part of town that Andy did not know well: near the railroad tracks, on a street of run-down houses that seemed to squeak when you looked at them.... Maria... had four brothers and two sisters—all younger than she and all living with their mother in four crowded rooms. Her father had died the year before in a mill accident. Her mother worked in a cafe on the same street... a small tired woman who had nothing to say.

Fortunately for Maria—not to mention Andy and the linear development of the story—she is qualified to attend any one of "at least a dozen colleges...on full scholarship," a fact which satisfies the requirements of the transformation motif and opens the path to solution and denouement. In short Andy is the conventional fair-haired boy, a flat character but nevertheless a cultural symbol that speaks of clean-cut, all-American puberty. He is immediately recognized by the readers of *Good Housekeeping* because he shares and is heroized by their culture. Maria for her part is a Cinderella, an equally flat and conventional figure who though fraught with adversity passes the ritual test and receives the culture's endorsement.

Viewed from the perspective of its characters then the short story is not simply a linear arrangement of bundles and motifs; it is also a set of polar oppositions. Thus a second morphological pattern emerges, a pattern whose structure is binary:

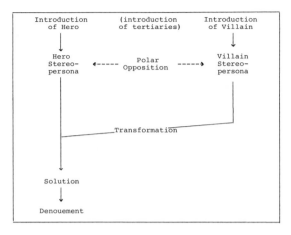

The Binary Structure of the Short Short Story

Now the focus has shifted. Now linear arrangements become secondary and the most important characteristic of the structure is its binary opposition. The critical elements of the story, whatever their order of appearance, are the rival value sets represented by heroes and villains. Indeed so crucial is the binary nature of the fable that the competition must always occur between what can usefully be called *stereopersonas*, each one a character so conventional in its attributes that it is a cultural cliche. Each fable swirls around opposing stereopersonas: Andy the white-Anglo-Saxon-Protestant v. the dark, probably Roman Catholic Maria from across the tracks; Mary (the plain Jane) Nickerson v. her sister the prima donna; the all-American male v. the continental rakehell; the punctual husband v. the tardy wife; Mom&Dad&Bud&Sis v. the lonely spinster; the poor-little-rich-girl v. the fallen woman; and so on.

But if conflict is the key the binary structure never lays waste to the linear, and conflict therefore is never severe enough to jeopardize solution and denouement. Most polarities are more apparent than real. Thus Maria will go to college with the waspy, wealthy Andy, and career girls given half the chance dissolve into happy homemakers. The tardy wife is punctual when the chips are down, and the lonely spinster, abrasive and irascible at first, becomes the neighborly grandmother with the bottomless cookie jar once Bud&Sis work their adolescent wiles on her. Occasionally an authentic polarity is established but even that can be quickly scuttled via the vanishing-villainy variant. Always, as before, the "future [is] safe. In his strong hands." Or to quote again from the larger tradition: they lived happily after.

So the fable whether ancient or modern is understood primarily in terms of its structure. It is however understood in this manner not merely architecturally but morally. For when it is finally asked: what systems of morality are proffered by these little fables?—it is once again the structure that holds the answer.

The world of the modern fable is to be sure a world of conflict, a world in which polar oppositions are quite literally built into everyone's life. But between 1965 and 1970, years now remembered for the critical conflict and dissension that they brought to the United States, polarities in *Good Housekeeping* were remarkably bland. Though an unpopular war was raging in Vietnam only once in fifty-two stories is there mention of the fact.* Although crime rates in America had reached new peaks, crime like war finds its way into only one contribution. And though poverty in America had become a concern of national proportions, on only three occasions do these fables by *Good Housekeeping* turn on issues of economics, and those moreover concentrate on the professional or economic problems of the middle class. Instead most of the situations treated by these stories are personal in nature: courtship and marriage, family and friends. And here too no problem is too great for solution.

One compelling explanation for this easy solubility is the amazing homogeneity of the stories' characters. The

*In "Good-bye-Too Soon" by Leonhard Dowty *(Good Housekeeping,* October 1969, pp. 118), the hero is drafted and subsequently killed in Vietnam. This turn of events is so catastrophic that the basic structure of the genre is violated, making "Good-bye-Too Soon" in this structural sense not a short short story.

hero more often than not is a woman, usually a young woman and typically a homemaker, career girl, or student. If male the hero is usually executive: junior grade. And whatever the gender heroes are invariably white and typically middle class. Significantly the demographics of villainy are similar to those of heroism. Villains too are usually young adults. They are more frequently women, never nonwhite—though quaintly enough occasionally of Mediterranean stock—and involved in the same variety of middle-class occupations as their heroic counterparts. Tertiary characters in their turn merely repeat the pattern.

In short wherever one looks the image is so many swatches cut from a single bolt of cloth. Homogeneity in this literally fabulous population far exceeds that of the so-called "melting pot" or "salad bowl" society in which it is set. Indeed it far exceeds the homogeneity to be found among the readers of the fables, for according to market research between 1965 and 1970 nearly ten percent of *Good Housekeeping*'s readership was nonwhite and nearly sixty percent belonged to the "working classes" as distinct from the white middle class that dominates the fables.[7]

Kind of Problem	Percentage
Personal Relations	
Courtship	14.3%
Marriage	34.7
Family	32.7
Friends	8.2
Total	89.8%
Economic & Professional	6.1
Crime	2.0
War	2.0

Problems within the Short Short Story

Whatever the explanation the basic moral pattern in these stories is not conflict in any usual sense so much as conflict within consensus, gentle struggle among the like-minded, and temporary debate within preordained unanimity. R.W. Alexander, one of the more successful of modern fablists, gives it all away in his advice to novice writers. The heart of the short short story he says is:

> some problem or situation that... has to be settled right away.... It is an important thing, this problem they [the characters] have to solve. It has a direct bearing on their happiness.... It is something big in their lives, though they may take only a few moments to get it straightened out.... It won't come up again, or certainly not in the same form. This is one hurdle they've got over safely, and they feel the better for it.

Alexander who understands the didactic nature of this genre concludes the lesson by saying that "we can only hope the reader feels better for it, too. He should, if the story has been well done."[8]

This pattern of struggle and solution is of course the moral analogue of the genre's morphological patterns, both linear (which presumes not only problems but resolutions) and binary (in which polar oppositions are set up but quickly knocked down). Thus the didactic content of the modern fable is as conventional, as completely a cultural cliche, as the stereopersonas which give it life. The moral system implicit in these short short stories is consonant with that found at mid-century by the anthropologist Cora DuBois. "For the American middle class," she wrote in 1955, "it is postulated that: 1) the universe is mechanistically conceived, 2) man is its master, 3) men are equal, and 4) men are perfectible."[9] The world of *Good Housekeeping* , need it be said, is the demographic and moral equivalent of DuBois' middle America. The Newtonian mechanistics, the egalitarianism, the buoyance and optimism: it is all here. To quote one of Alexander's own denouement clauses:

Demographic Variables	Hero	Villain	Tertiary
Age:			
Child	10.0%	6.3%	14.3%
Teenager	10.0	6.3	7.1
Young Adult	52.0	54.2	57.1
Middle Aged	28.0	31.3	21.4
Old Aged	0.0	2.1	0.0
Sex:			
Male	36.2	26.7	46.4
Female	40.4	51.1	42.9
2+*	23.4	22.2	10.7
Race:			
Anglo-Saxon	97.6	91.4	82.1
Mediterranean	2.4	8.6	3.6
Other	0.0	0.0	0.0
Occupation (number of occurrences)	Executive (17)	Executive (9)	Executive (8)
	Housewife (9)	Housewife (7)	Housewife (5)
	Student (4)	Career Girl (5)	Student (4)
	Career Girl (3)	Student (2)	
	Businessman (2)	Worker (2)	
		Artist (1)	
		Pensioner (1)	

*2+ refers to heterosexual groups of persons--usually couples or families--who serve as heroes, villains, or tertiaries.

The Demography of the Short Short Story

"Everything," she told him, feeling with all of her being the truth of what she was saying.

"Everything's fine."[10]

The trouble of course is that everything *isn't* fine. Polarities in *Good Housekeeping* are easily dissolved because the real polarities are fastidiously ignored. Where are the marriages that deserve to fail? Where are the people whose politics fall to the left of Carter or the right of IKE? Where are the kids who refuse to conform? And where are the ethnics, the Jews, the Slavs and the Greeks, the Asians, the Indians, and the blacks? Is it not interesting that in analyzing these fables one finds useful racial distinctions only by regressing to quaint notions of Nordic superiority and Mediterranean inferiority? But this too is part of the fable form. Fair-haired lads and dark-eyed Cinderellas are not real, of course, not at any rate as perfected by *Good Housekeeping*'s short short stories. But then neither is Reynard the Fox or Br'er Rabbit. Rather they function didactically. They dramatize the great middle American mind set and bid us conform that we might be accorded righteous.

Didactic journalism did not begin with modern women's magazines. If D.H. Lawrence is to be believed it was an earlier journalist, Ben Franklin, who "set up the first dummy American.... Now wasn't that an American thing to do?" *Good Housekeeping* merely maintains the tradition, constructing dummies in our image that we may build our lives on theirs.

Six

Magazine:
How Playboy *Was Politicized*

*I*f you're a man between the ages of 18 and 80, *Playboy* is meant for you."

Thus assured the editors in the December, 1953, inaugural issue of a magazine billed as "Entertainment for Men." A dubious venture at best, no publication date or volume number appear on the cover: just the price (50¢), a photograph of Marilyn Monroe in full decolletage, and the noncommittal statistic "1st issue." A dubious venture, but it worked. Though its initial effort was a forty-page paste-up of tasteless pictures and old reprints from Boccaccio and Sherlock Holmes *Playboy* was destined for success. In an era that witnessed the failure of many an established magazine—*Look* and *Life, Collier's* and *Saturday Evening Post* come to mind—*Playboy* grew to enjoy a circulation in excess of five million, becoming the eleventh largest periodical in America. Moreover the magazine became the flagship of an empire containing supper clubs and resort hotels, television programs, motion pictures and a book club, and even a small air force. Its name and symbol—the ubiquitous bunny rabbit—came to stand for an ethos, a lifestyle, an ethical system so complete that inevitably it required Harvey Cox, a theologian, to illuminate what he called the "doctrine of male," a doctrine that explains "what it means to be a *man*, and more specifically a *male*, in today's world."[1] *Playboy*, in short, has become a bit of Americana, known and recognized, and alternately loved or vilified, across the country and throughout the world.

But more than success and fame have come to *Playboy*; politics has come to *Playboy*. The "Entertainment for Men" that its editor, Hugh Hefner, had originally intended to be "served up with humor, sophistication and spice," with "[a]ffairs of state...out of our province," has become an overtly political magazine. Its content radically expanded to encompass an open treatment of political issues and to express an explicitly political point of view, *Playboy* has become a periodical of public opinion. Given the avowedly apolitical convictions with which it was conceived and the high status in the newstands which it presently enjoys, the question begs to be asked: when and how was *Playboy* politicized?

That *Playboy* was born innocent of public affairs is beyond all argument. *"Playboy* will emphasize entertainment," said the early editorial policy:

> Affairs of state will be out of our province. We don't expect to solve any world problems or prove any great moral truths. If we are able to give the American male a few extra laughs and a little diversion from the anxieties of the Atomic Age, we'll feel we've justified our existence.[2]

And divert it did. In its first sixty-five issues *Playboy* published nothing of an explicitly political nature. Seven articles, less than one percent of the total, addressed issues conceivably political, but only if the term were to be given its widest possible definition.

In the issue for June, 1959, readers found an article on "The Mann Act." A fitting debut upon the world of public opinion given the subject's sexual overtones, "The Mann Act" was the first explicitly political article to appear in *Playboy* and the beginning of a faint vein of politically-oriented content that would run through the next forty months. Ralph Ginzburg for instance appeared with an essay on "The Cult of the Aged Leader," and other contributors followed with articles on taxes, censorship and drug enforcement. Two "Playboy Panels" were convened, one on "Sex and Censorship in Literature and the Arts," the other on "The Womanization of America." And the social critic Nat Hentoff appeared with an essay entitled "Through the Racial Looking Glass," a prescient account of growing militancy and separatism within America's black community. But public issues remained a minor vein in *Playboy*. Quantitatively political articles made up less than two percent of the total content. In terms of quality the thrust was tangential, the topics really only quasi-political. Perhaps the tone was most honestly expressed by the editors themselves in "The Contaminators." Reciting the perils of Strontium 90 and the resultant radiation, they admitted that the commentary:

> is an odd message to be appearing in a magazine dedicated, as *Playboy* is, to life's good things. But these good things, this joy and fun, will cease to exist if life itself ceases to exist. And that is precisely what may happen.[3]

Public issues ought not be completely ignored, they seemed to be saying, lest some crisis arise to play hob with *joie de vivre*.

Still there it was: *Playboy* had crept away from its silence on politics and public life. And as it completed its first decade the magazine expanded further to include interviews with major political figures, articles on major political issues, and moreover an overt political position of its own. The politization process began slowly but acceleration away from the early pleasure-primer principle was swift. In 1962 "The Playboy Philosophy" series was inaugurated, and in the following year the magazine hit a political stride that it would retain. Suddenly from virtually nothing ten and fifteen percent of *Playboy*, the erstwhile eschewer of such matters, was devoted to public issues. Only journals of an avowed advocacy could boast more.

"The Playboy Philosophy" was itself of small importance. Begun in December, 1962, and sprinkled rather

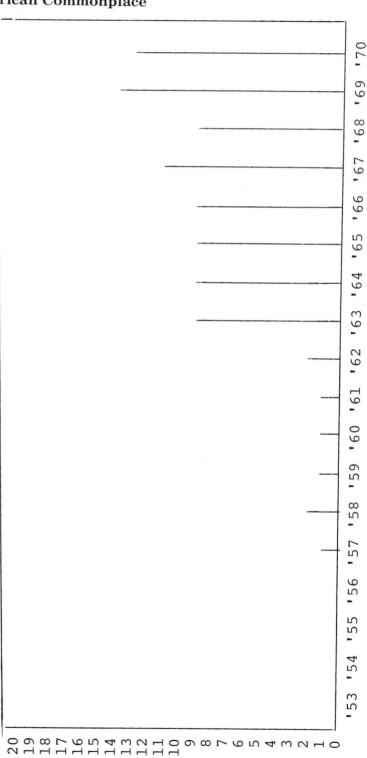

6.2
The Politization of *Playboy*

irregularly through subsequent issues, the "Philosophy" was intended to restate—while interestingly enough also contradict—"our own editorial credo...and offer a few personal observations on our present-day society and *Playboy*'s part in it."[4] More a rumination than a philosophy, the series quickly degenerated into a discussion of sexual mores, with the editor Hefner decrying America's Victorian attitudes toward adultery, sodomy, homosexuality, pornography and the like. Intended for organs considerably lower than the cerebrum the "Philosophy" was nevertheless an important landmark in *Playboy*'s politization. First the series was an extended effort as Hefner put it to "offer... observations on our present-day society," and if the series subsequently fell to crypto-erotic levels the political motives remained apparent. Moreover when the "Philosophy" did on occasion rise to cerebral heights Hefner's ideological position became explicit. It was not a surprising stance given the affluent and upper-middle class nature of *Playboy's* constituency. He spoke at length of the "Uncommon Man" and of the necessity of maintaining a system that leaves him unfettered. He sang the essential goodness of elitism in politics and of free enterprise in economics, claiming that the "acquisition of property is the cornerstone of our American economic system."[5] Throughout the series Hefner came off sounding like a sensual robber baron, the issue if you will of a tryst between Andrew Carnegie and this month's "playmate": conservative, acquisitive, materialistic, libertarian, ardent, egoistic and of course sexy.

Following the "Philosophy" came another series important to the politization of *Playboy*: "The Playboy Forum" initiated in July, 1963. Originally a column of readers' response to the "Philosophy," this second series was destined to continue as a regular feature of *Playboy* long after the "Philosophy" itself had lapsed into irregularity. In the late 1960s and 1970s the "Forum" published opinions on a host of subjects, virtually all of them political, few of them raised by the "Philosophy."

If in the "Forum" *Playboy* had sired its most regularly and durably political feature, simultaneously another and even more important change, as has been noted, was taking place: a marked increase in the amount of coverage given to public affairs. In purely statistical terms while the tenth issue for 1962 had no political content the fifth and eighth issues for 1963 were respectively eleven and thirteen percent political, the eleventh issue a whopping twenty-four percent. Qualitatively the magazine was moving toward and into the 1970s along a number of interesting paths, all of them leading away from the original pleasure-primer principle.

Item. "The Playboy Panel" discussions mentioned earlier now moved to "The Crisis in Law Enforcement," "The Student Revolt"—this in September, 1969, eight months before the infamous Kent State firings—and "The Drug Revolution." A variation on the "Panel" format was the occasional "compendium" or "symposium," a group of articles on a single public issue. An example from early 1963 is "The Role of the Right Wing in America Today," featuring contrasting essays by William F. Buckley, Jr. and Norman Mailer followed by a debate between the two essayists. At decade's end *Playboy* was publishing "The Decent Society," a symposium so political in content and reputable in tone that readers might understandably have thought themselves stumbled into the pages of *Saturday Review* or even *Daedalus:*

Foreign Affairs	*Theodore C. Sorensen*
Race Relations	*John V. Lindsay*
Equality & Opportunity	*Kenneth B. Clark*
The Physical Environment	*Peter Matthiessen*
Science & Technology	*Jerome B. Weisner*
Business	*Charles H. Percy*
Education	*William Sloane Coffin*
Communications	*Edward P. Morgan*
The Arts & Entertainment	*Kenneth Tynan*
Religion & Morality	*Harvey Cox*
Civil Liberties:	
The Crucial Issue	*Justice Wm. O. Douglas*

Other compendia followed with subjects such as "Bring Us Together" (with articles by George McGovern, Cesar Chavez, Julian Bond and Tom Wicker), "The Chicago Conspiracy Circus... and the Legal Questions it Raises," and "A New Set of National Priorities" with the then U.S. Senator Gaylord Nelson writing on pollution, Cleveland's Mayor Carl B. Stokes on urbanization, and the socialist critic Michael Harrington on poverty.

Item. Another of the magazine's regular features, "The Playboy Interview," in the 1960s underwent permanent politization. Originally known as "Candid Conversation," the series had begun in September, 1962, by interviewing the famous jazz musician Miles Davis. A train of other entertainers followed—Peter Sellers, Jackie Gleason, Frank Sinatra—but after Sinatra came a philosopher and more important a pacifist: Bertrand Russell. A new trend began with the Russell interview, for while entertainers and others continued to be featured, the personality of "The Playboy Interview" oftener than not was a man or woman of public affairs. In its second decade *Playboy* interviewed dignitaries both foreign (e.g., Fidel Castro and Jawaharlal Nehru) and domestic (George McGovern, Charles Percy and George Wallace); thinkers to the right (William F. Buckley Jr., H.L. Hunt, Madalyn Murray, Ayn Rand, George Lincoln Rockwell and Robert Shelton), to the left (Joan Baez, Ramsey Clark, William Sloane Coffin, John Kenneth Galbraith, William Kunstler, Ralph Nader, Arthur Schlesinger, Jr., Norman Thomas and Gore Vidal), and up above (Allen Ginsberg and Timothy Leary); political satirists (Art Buchwald and Al Capp); racial activists (Mohammad Ali [then Cassius Clay], Eldridge Cleaver, Charles Evers, Dick Gregory, Jesse Jackson, Martin Luther King, Jr. and Malcolm X); labor leaders (James Hoffa) and birth control advocates (Mary Calderone) and others (John V. Lindsay, Norman Mailer and Albert Speer).

Item. After 1963 *Playboy* published not only composia and interviews of a political nature but regularly featured independent articles and essays on a range of public affairs.

Thus its readers were offered William O. Douglas, Julian Huxley, Gene Marine and Robert Sherrill on ecology; discussions of international affairs by Frank Church, J. William Fulbright, John Kenneth Galbraith, David Halberstam, Max Lerner, Bertrand Russell and Norman Thomas; James Baldwin and Vine Deloria on minorities; and opinions on civil liberties by Peter Andrews, Thomas B. Curtis, Arthur Goldberg, Jacob Javits, Edward V. Long and Stephen M. Young. Mike Royko appeared with "Hizzoner," an article on the then Chicago Mayor Richard Daley; Michael DiSalle and Vance Hartke contributed opinions on law and order; and articles on ideology appeared by Bruno Bettelheim, Richard Flacks, James Kavanaugh and Jack Newfield.

One cannot read such stuff without musing upon the promise of *Playboy*'s inaugural issue: "Affairs of state will be out of our province." But *Playboy* did not simply become cognizant of its readers' political world; it moved beyond "Entertainment for Men" and beyond "affairs of state" to assume an ideological position from which to view those "affairs of state." Some clues to that position can be had by scanning the magazine's contents. The authors of the politically oriented articles, the subjects chosen for symposia, the attitudes of readers as expressed in the "Forum," and the persons chosen for the "Interview": the spectrum is wide but the taste is unmistakably left-of-center. Liberals are read for instructional purposes, fringes to the far left are taken seriously, and the radical right is jollied with.* Moreover these clues, subjective though they be, are nicely corroborated by a hard piece of objective data that *Playboy* presented during the election campaign of 1970: "Playboy's Political Preference Chart."

Billed as "a thumbnail election guide, rating this year's congressional and gubernatorial candidates according to their views and voting records on the key issues," the chart

*Notably it was *Playboy* that sent Alex Haley, the black author of *The Autobiography of Malcolm X,* to interview the fascist and avowed racist George Lincoln Rockwell.

Incumbents	Ratings			Incumbents	Ratings		
	ADA*	Playboy*	ACA+		ADA*	Playboy*	ACA+
Senate				House			
Murphy (Calif.)	3	27	81	Udall (Ariz.)	76	72	0
Dodd (Conn.)	16	64	81	Rouselot (Calif.)	29	29	100
Hartke (Ind.)	66	86	21	Goldwater (Calif.)	0	43	88
Muskie (Maine)	91	72	10	Pucinski (Ill.)	48	29	26
Tydings (Md.)	63	72	12	Landgrebe (Ind.)	12	29	100
Kennedy (Mass.)	84	93	5	Sebelius (Kan.)	8	50	82
Hart (Mich.)	97	93	9	Ford (Mich.)	12	43	68
Williams (N.J.)	94	86	5	Symington (Mo.)	72	72	24
Goodell (N.Y.)	97	86	5	Olsen (Mont.)	84	86	21
Gore (Tenn.)	53	86	25	Howard (N.J.)	76	86	11
Moss (Utah)	69	64	3	Helstoski (N.J.)	96	86	6
Prouty (Vt.)	34	43	50	Lowenstein (N.Y.)	100	93	22
Byrd (Va.)	22	29	87	Chisholm (N.Y.)	80	93	25
McGee (Wyo.)	47	50	32	McKneally (N.Y.)	16	64	44
				Stratton (N.Y.)	48	50	21
				Button (N.Y.)	64	72	21
				Preyer (N.C.)	40	50	37
				Ayres (Ohio)	20	43	31
				Stokes (Ohio)	96	86	18

*100 = perfect liberalism
+100 = perfect conservatism

Sources: "Playboy's Political Preference Chart," op. cit.; Congressional Quarterly Weekly Report,
Vol. 29, April 16, 1971, pp. 865-67.

"Playboy's Political Preference Chart."
Courtesy Playboy Enterprises

was a guide to voting not unlike those published by more renowned organs of ideology such as the Americans for Democratic Action or the American Conservative Union. Also like these other charts *Playboy*'s guide reveals as much about the raters as it does about the rated.

Playboy evaluated thirty-nine senatorial candidates, forty-two candidates for the House of Representatives, and six of the more well-known gubernatorial hopefuls. Each was appraised against four of the day's substantive issues: "peace," "civil rights," "individual liberties" and "pollution of environment."* The data on which *Playboy* based its evaluations, obtained from the offices of *Congressional Quarterly*, were presumably non-partisan. The chart itself however was overtly ideological. "*Playboy*'s own judgments and convictions," the editors frankly admitted, "pervade the charts." And what were those jugments and convictions as they pertained to the four selected issues?

On "peace":

> ...nothing to be gained by the prosecution of the Vietnam war is worth the cost.

On "civil rights":

> ...blacks and other minority groups have not reached full equality in America... present laws and Executive leadership remain inadequate.

On "individual liberties":

> ...we support each person's right... as set forth in the Bill of Rights, not as many lawmakers would prefer to interpret them. And we are especially appalled at the present trend of writing laws to increase the unrestrained use of police power at the cost of individual liberty.

The fourth issue posed a more subtle problem, since *Playboy* thought:

*The candidates were also judged on what *Playboy* called "stature."

...no politician would be foolish enough to take a stand against stopping pollution. Our estimate of each candidate's ecological attitude, therefore, is an attempt to judge his forthrightness and dedication as well as his proclaimed position.

Pledged to these convictions and armed with the appropriate paraphernalia—voting records, candidate statements, biographical sketches, questionnaire responses—*Playboy* proceeded to grade the politicians on a five-point scale ranging from "A" through "F." Among the senatorial candidates receiving an overall grade of "A" were Edward Kennedy, Wisconsin's Philip Hart, and New York's Richard Ottinger. A half step below in the "A-" category were Indiana's Vance Hartke (described in *Playboy* as "a feisty anti-war liberal"); Harrison Williams, Jr., the Democratic incumbent from New Jersey ("pro-labor dove"); New York's Charles Goodell (who, said *Playboy*, "takes big risks to out-Bobby [Kennedy] Bobby's memory"); and the late Albert Gore of Tennessee ("a courtly anti-war populist... number one on Ted Agnew's black list"). At the nether pole of *Playboy*'s senatorial preference chart were the likes of Harry F. Byrd, Jr., of Virginia, a "hawkish, conservative product of Byrdland"; and Texas' Lloyd Bentsen who seemed at the time to be a "hip-shooting hawk who doesn't like blacks, Mexicans or kids."

Among the prominent congressional aspirants rated by *Playboy* was Senator Goldwater's son Barry, Jr., who received a "C-," a grade that was also assigned to Gerald Ford, then House Republican leader and future thirty-eighth President of the United States. Receiving an "A" or an "A-" were the late Allard Lowenstein, liberal Democrat from New York; liberal, Democratic, black and female Shirley Chisholm; and Louis Stokes, Democratic and black brother of Cleveland's Carl. *Playboy*'s taste in gubernatorial candidates followed suit. John Gilligan, the "bright, concerned idealist" who was successful in Ohio, was awarded an "A-." Former Supreme Court Justice Arthur Goldberg received a "B." And Ronald Reagan on his way from the movies to the White House received a thumping "D-."[6]

Such were the inclinations of "Playboy's Political Preference Chart": dovish in foreign affairs, integrationist in race relations, left-of-center on individual liberties, and opposed to environmental pollution. Clearly then *Playboy* had moved beyond the pleasure-primer principle, beyond the coverage of political affairs, and to the left of Hefner's own "Philosophy," to develop an ideological stance as obvious as that of the *National Review* or the *New Republic*. In politics as in success and fame, *Playboy* had come a long way from that "1st issue" in 1953.

And so it was that *Playboy* became a journal of swank but liberal opinion in America. In doing so *Playboy* in the deepest figurative sense came of age. *Playboy* ceased to be simply another girlie magazine. It ceased even to be simply a manual of arms for the young man-about-town. That it had been such a manual is unassailable. It was precisely this point that Cox had spoken to in his essay on "*Playboy*'s Doctrine of Male." "For the insecure young man with newly acquired time and money on his hands who still feels uncertain about his consumer skills, *Playboy* supplies a comprehensive and authoritative guidebook," Cox argued, telling "him not only who to be... [but] *how* to be it." And the critic Benjamin DeMott had made the same and other points in his essay on "The Anatomy of 'Playboy'." But the politization of *Playboy* called the critics into serious question. The crux of their dismissal of *Playboy* after all was *Playboy*'s dismissal of the real world. For Cox the magazine projected a "synthetic doctrine of man," and therefore was merely the "latest and slickest episode in man's continuing refusal to be fully human."[7] And for DeMott matters were even seamier. "The *Playboy* world," he wrote:

> is first and last an achievement in abstraction: history, politics, art, ordinary social relations, religion, families, nature, vanity, love, a thousand other items that presumably complicate the... lives of human beings—all have been emptied from it. In place of the citizen with a vote to cast or a job to do or a book to study or a god to

worship, the editors offer a vision of the whole man reduced to his private parts. Out of the center of his being spring the only substantial realities—sexual need and sexual deprivation.[8]

And as if to continue the denial of *Playboy*'s politization critics continued into the 1970s to think in primarily genital terms. Thus Peter Schrag in *The Decline of the Wasp* quarantined *Playboy* to a world of "sex and gadgets [that] will, by themselves, represent all the answers to a man's prayers," with women "presented as objects of consumption roughly on a par with tape recorders, lounge jackets, cologne and sports cars."[9]

It has however become a stale criticism. Whatever erstwhile merits it may have enjoyed, the processes of politization have severely compromised its validity. Today's *Playboy* is neither empty of politics nor unaware of the world beyond its penthouse. It has become at the very least a more sophisticated manual—to use Cox's terms a final time—of "what it means to be a man...in today's world." *Playboy* has become, Hugh Hefner might say, a magazine for the compleat man: compleat at least with an eye for the political and a taste for the ideological.

Seven

Academy:
Notes in Brownian Motion

Well before his death in 1980 it had become axiomatic that Marshall McLuhan's *Understanding Media* could not be understood. The book itself defies comprehension and the many compendia, bowdlerizations, and composia that came to make sense of the nonsense served only to verify his unintelligibility. This has since its publication in 1964 been disturbing to educated men and women who have clawed through weighty stuff: James Joyce, say, or Norman O. Brown. Perturbing as it is and past success notwithstanding, many readers cannot "dig" Marshall McLuhan.

The real culprit of course is not the reader's inability so much as it is *Understanding Media* itself. McLuhan's most important literary remains has been aptly described as "a viscous fog, through which loom stumbling metaphors," and this style—this medium—is the message.[1] His writing cannot be followed, so to speak, because he did not lead. *Understanding Media* illustrates what it prophesied: the decline of linear composition. "Scholars today," he noted, "are acutely aware of a discrepancy between their ways of treating subjects and the subject itself.... While their treatment must be linear, the subject is not." Books, he meant to say, have been linear not because their subjects consist of causes and effects, evolutions and unfoldings; books have been linear because the printed page is a linear medium and the medium requires a story line.

But even as McLuhan drew no lines McLuhan's readers follow no lines. They simply view the book, waiting for metaphors to loom. Entertaining few qualms as they ignore whole sections, they take assurance from the book itself that "one can stop anywhere after the first few sentences and have the full message, if one is prepared to 'dig' it."[2] Nor was the professor alone in his rejection of linear forms. Even as he predicted the age of the non-linear message came to be. From every cranny of experience electronic impulses arrived to jerk and jar us. The blip replaced the saga; a stack of random "45s" replaced the symphony. Gone the waltz, come the St. Vitus dance. The story that would have been played out in lines and themes now emerged as a montage of jerks and starts. Viscous fog was everywhere. Metaphors stumbled and richocheted in brownian motion.* A moment of new composition had arrived. Coming out, as we shall see, of the popular culture, it was ushered by McLuhan as much as anyone into the academy, altering the discourse of learned men and women. How and to what result that alteration is worth examining.

The precise distinctions between linear and brownian compositions have been on vivid display in the popular media, particularly in television programming and

---

Brownian motion a phenomenon named after the Scottish scientist Robert Brown, is defined as "the peculiar random movement exhibited by microscopic particles...when suspended in liquids or gases." The textbooks describe it as "a continuous irregular motion," a "random molecular bombardment," and the "irregular zigzag movement of extremely minute particles." It is a phenomenon known too well by the readers of *Understanding Media*.

advertising. The oldstyle in comedy for instance is linear. *Situation comedy* they call it, meaning that the humor is contextual. It flows not from any intrinsic quality in the punch line so much as from the irony or anomaly or malapropism of the situation. Be it Lucille Ball in the 1950s or Archie Bunker in the '70s they are funny mainly within the context of their programming. They set themselves up, so to speak, only to knock themselves down. The brownian style by contrast is devoid of situation. *Laugh-In* for example, which was so popular on American television in the 1970s, and its country cousin *Hee Haw* which retained its popularity into the '80s are a happening without context. The technique is non-linear. Discrete molecules of humor bombard the viewers, tickling them again and again until they are convulsed in a fit of laughter. BAM!—a silly little Nazi lurks behind the bushes—BAM!—a flock of cartoon chickens scurry across the screen—BAM!—a martini-sipping Episcopalian priest promiscuously paraphrases the Ninth Commandment—BAM!—a bikini-clad Negress dances the frug, "Sock it to me!" painted on her thigh, or Minnie Pearl takes fifteen seconds to relate an old Vaudeville gag—Bam! No context, no situation, no continuity; merely an incongruous barrage of tickling ricochets.

Linear composition and brownian motion have been on equally vivid display in television commercial advertising. The oldstyle commercial with its "before" and "after" frames is necessarily linear:

Frame One: protagonist fails in relations with peers;
Frame Two: on advice from friend protagonist uses sponsor's product (mouthwash, coffee, shampoo, girdle, aspirin);
Frame Three: protagonist succeeds in relations with peers.

Like the situation comedy that it often sponsors, the old-style commercial is contextual. Only in sequence do the frames make sense; out of sequence they baffle or even insult. But brownian advertising like brownian programming is colloidal. Notice particularly that the commercial which sells a soft drink is more often than not a montage of vaguely related film clips: child sailing a model boat—lovers at fireside—teenagers at a drag race—father and daughter lifting a kite into a March wind—dusty road leaping down a rural lane or sun reflected from a skyscraper's windows—grandma in apron on Thanksgiving Day. To be sure there is a message: "Coke is Life" and the "Pepsi generation" is "comin' at ya'." But the medium is one that McLuhan helped us to understand. Thus even as the newstyle comics bombard their viewers with thousands of jabs and tickles, so the brownian commercial bathes them in soothing and attractive imagery.

Situation comedies and Listerine commercials and other oldstyle compositions differ then in several critical respects from, say, *Hee Haw* or a Pepsi Cola commercial or some other piece of McLuhanism. Oldstyle is linear; newstyle is brownian. Oldstyle is constructed of introductions, climaxes, and conclusions and is nothing if not the sequential sum of its parts; newstyle is formed in random disarray, with spasm and flux. And finally oldstyle obliges the audience to be attentive, to follow the story, to seek the conclusion and win the message. But since the brownian motion makes no such demands the audience can, as McLuhan wrote, "stop anywhere after the first few sentences and have the full message, if one is prepared to 'dig' it."

The cultural invasion of brownian motion would be worth noting even if its impact were limited to the mass media and the popular mind. But since McLuhan's *Understanding Media* and continuing into the 1970s at least, the newstyle has found its way into elite culture: into the classroom and lecture hall, into literary criticism, historical explication, and other scholarly endeavors. This latter invasion has done more than merely tickle ribs or sell mouthwash. That the newstyle would infiltrate the media of elites is absolutely noteworthy for the brownian medium—

which of course means also the brownian message—is in many ways contrary to the purpose of rational men and women. Notice nevertheless the impact of the new composition upon the cultivated mind:

Media	Linear Composition	Brownian Composition
Television programming	(situation comedy)	Laugh-in
Television advertising	Listerine	Pepsi-Cola
Social Commentary	Joseph Wood Krutch	Marshall McLuhan
Literature		
1) creative	O'Henry	James Joyce
2) critical	Robert Spiller	Ojab Jassam
History	Allan Nevins	Norman Mailer
Pedagogy		
1) lecture	(the sermon)	Marshall Fishwick
2) seminar	Leopold von Ranke	Neil Postman and Charles Weingartner
3) A-V	motion pictures	slides

Linear Media and Brownian Motion

What, one might ask, is the common denominator among the social critic Joseph Wood Krutch, the author O'Henry, the literary critic Robert Spiller, the historians Allan Nevins and Leopold von Ranke, the media sermons and motion pictures? And what would that common denominator have to do with Listerine commericals and situation comedies? At least this much: each is a devotee of the straight line and accordingly all superimpose a special kind of order on their subjects. Nevins' confession is the clearest of them. In his *Gateway to History* he described his discipline as:

the sextant of states which, tossed by wind and current, would be lost in confusion if they could not fix their position.

History enables bewildered bodies of human beings to grasp their relationship with their past, and helps them chart on general lines their immediate forward course.

The craft of the historian then is for Nevins to make order, to make of the past a lantern that will illuminate the "predicament and prospects" of peoples and nations that are "harried and perplexed by the sweep of events."[3]

Matters are not significantly different in creative or critical literature, in social commentary, or in pedagogy. The purpose of persons engaged in such callings has traditionally been to make sense, linear sense, of their subjects. Thus Krutch's editorials, in, say, *The American Scholar* took their unconscious cues from the apocryphal black evangelist whose rules of the sermon were:

> First I tells 'em what I'z guine tell 'em;
> Then I tells 'em;
> Then I tells 'em what I'z done tol' 'em.

Krutch's work was that pristine, a model of that clarity. He was, as they say, easy to follow, which means of course that he was linear.

So was O'Henry whose short stories American high school students still dissect into exposition, plot, climax, and denouement—a sequence by the way that O'Henry shares with Listerine. Or Robert Spiller of Spiller, *et. al.*, whose *Literary History of the United States* is not only standard but symmetrical and sequential, mammoth and inexorable in its unfolding. Or von Ranke, the father of the Prussian seminar, in whose scenario each student is weaving in a corner, each corner a part of the tapestry, history finally of whole cloth, all reasonable and orderly. It is so like a motion picture this linear stuff: several hundred feet of celluloid unwinding over the lens and telling the story in integrated, sequential, linear patterns. And it is so very unlike the brownian motion.

Contrast for instance the essays of Krutch with, say, McLuhan's early volume *The Mechanical Bride*. Written in 1951 *Mechanical Bride* is a rhetorical fricassee, a dismembered cluster of comments on the world of commercial advertising, a random mosaic of pieces disguised as chapters. The first piece, "Front Page," is instructive of the whole. A newspaper McLuhan said is discontinuity in print, a random montage of "coverage from China to Peru." But he saw a fascinating orchestration in the front page. Its stories, quite unrelated either to each other or to the story of the reader, nevertheless "are abruptly overlayered in cubist or Picasso style to provide a greatly enriched image."[4] Eighteen years later McLuhan made the same point in *Playboy* magazine: "News items are necessarily unconnected except by a date line," he said. "The newspaper mosaic has no story line. Like syncopated jazz or poetic symbolism, it is discontinuous."[5] So is *Mechanical Bride* and *Understanding Media* and the rest of McLuhan's literary remains. Random notions in colloidal suspension.

Or contrast the literary criticism of Spiller's *LHUS* with the work of the critic Ihab Hassan. Hassan is not much interested in linear critics, for he is a revolutionary and, as he says, linear criticism belongs to the "party of Memory" (a phrase incidentally which was popularized by the linear critic R.W.B. Lewis). Their work lags behind the literature of its day, which itself lags behind its day. Instead he is interested in a literature of "Magic Theatre.... How about a trip," he inquires, "that will dissolve the floors of memory and identity, becloud the boundaries separating reality and illusion, return the traveler momentarily to his primal, psychic, self—all without benefit of hallucinogens."[6] This is Hassan's trip, his exegesis. Witness his "Silence, Revolution, and Consciousness." He begins:

Introduction

Silence, Revolution, and Consciousness: three parts. I begin in the middle.

...but he really does not, for there is no middle, end, or parts. Hassan is off on a fluid journey, forgetting language. "The next logical step," he says—quoting appropriately Marshall McLuhan—"would seem to be... to bypass language in favor of a general cosmic consciousness."[7]

In history the instructive contrast is between, say, Nevins' *Grover Cleveland* and Norman Mailer's *Armies of the Night* or *Miami and the Siege of Chicago*. Published in 1932 the central figure in Nevins' *Cleveland* is of course Cleveland. But the protagonist of *Armies of the Night* is outrageously Norman Mailer, "a figure of monumental disproportions... serv[ing] willy-nilly as the bridge" into the event. Mailer cannot be Nevins, cannot write a history that like Nevins' will enable "bewildered bodies of human beings to grasp their relationship with their past." He refuses, that is, to cloak chaos in the guise of order, convinced instead that history is a crazy house. And when an event takes place in the "crazy house of history it is fitting that any ambiguous comic hero of such a history should not be only off very much to the side of the history, but that he should be an egotist of the most startling misproportions." When history has no story line it will not do to sew in threads of mock order after the fact. Better to use the self-assertive lineament of an absurd observer. Better to trudge after the irrelevant Mr. Mailer as he wades through the spectacle. After all, "once History inhabits a crazy house, egotism may be the last tool left to History."[8]

In pedagogy the brownian motion has infected for instance the lectures of the American studies gadfly Marshall Fishwick. Fishwick is unique among lecturers because he has adopted a form widely assumed to be intrinsically linear and made it brownian. Watch him operate. His lecture notes are mini-thoughts, each on its individual index card. A fifty-minute lecture is forty or fifty cards. Another fifty-minute lecture: the same cards shuffled once. A twenty-minute lecture: half the stack chosen at random. The result is a mist of mini-thoughts, a McLuhanesque suspension of ideas/thoughts/feelings meant less for following than for bathing. And when Fishwick's lectures are supplemented by two slide projectors, a tape recording, and a motion picture projector the audience is caught in a cross fire of notions and emotions as they bounce and ricochet around the room.

But brownian pedagogy is also the seminar styles advocated by Neil Postman and Charles Weingartner, authors of *Teaching as a Subversive Activity*. An important artifact in the "relevance" revolution that swept through American education in the 1960s and '70s, *Teaching as a Subversive Activity* advocates a teaching strategy whose seminars are to von Ranke as *Finnegan's Wake* is to "The Ransom of Red Chief." Postman and Weingartner and the other exponents of "radical inquiry" advocate classrooms in which students are involved in the process of "meaning-making." Each student, that is to say, is learning how to make sense or meaning of the multifold stimuli around him or her. Each student is learning how to ask questions: not questions like "who discovered America?" but questions like "how do you discover who discovered America?" and—particularly for those with Christopher Columbus on their minds—"what do you mean by 'discover' anyway?" These advocates of radical inquiry believe that "once you have learned how to ask...relevant and appropriate questions... you have learned how to learn and no one can keep you from learning whatever you want or need to know." The seminars of Postman and Weingartner, it goes without saying, are disquieting to linear syllabus-and-textbook pedants, for the average syllabus is an oldstyle gadget that displays "someone else's story" and assumes that students will be mainly "covering the material." Subversive teaching on the other hand asks students to "work hard...at discovering patterns and assigning meanings to one's experiences. The focus of intellectual energy becomes the active investigation of structures and relationships." Within this anarchic context the only syllabus that will make sense is one that "tries to predict, account for, and deal with the authentic responses of learners to a particular problem."[9] It will be a most brownian syllabus even as the seminar will be a most colloidal experience.

Brownian fiction, finally, is the fiction of James Joyce. No one has ever been accused of following *Finnegan's Wake* although a veritable Joyce industry has labored for decades to lead them. One wonders why they bother, for it was Joyce himself who twitted the linear reader for being "abcedminded."

> (Stoop) [he would say] if you are abcedminded, to this claybook, what curios of sings (please stoop), in the allaphbed! Can you rede (since We and Thou had it already) its world?

It should be lost on no one why the Joycean notion of abc-ed-mindedness has been a favorite whipping post for McLuhan and the other brownians. Like them Joyce refused to be trussed into linearity. Instead he showed his readers the brownian motion and bid them delight to the "random molecular bombardment."

The extensions of brownian composition then, as McLuhan would have said, are global. If its expression in the mass media is clear its infiltration into high culture is also apparent. Further while brownian motion in the mass media may be merely interesting, the existence of non-linear culture forms is massive in its import and for this reason: the brownian motion diverges markedly from the oldstyle not only in its mode of communication but inevitably in its fundamental worldview. Elemental to wisdom before McLuhan was the assumption that chaos is order unperceived and that the cultured mind works to perceive the unperceived, clearly and with definition. But McLuhan's people have always suspected that order is really chaos in drag, and in any case clarity and definition are not on their minds. They would rather join with Emerson's "Nature" and stand...

> on the bare ground—my head bathed by the blithe air
> and uplifted into infinite space...I become a
> transparent eyeball; I am nothing; I see all; the currents
> of the Universal Being circulate through me; I am part
> and parcel of God.

Nor is it surprising, this affinity for transparent
eyeballs. Emerson after all was an oldtimer newstyler. And
the brownian motion is after all an upbeat
transcendentalism of sorts. The linear worldview is orderly
and *rational*, which the dictionary defines as "proceeding or
derived from reason or based on reasoning." But the
worldview of the brownians is irrational, religious, and
psychodelic, a word which means "intensely pleasureful
perception of the senses, esthetic entrancement, and creative
impetus." Thus Krutch's essays mirror, however
imperfectly, his rational universe and Nevins' history helps
peoples "grasp the relationship with their past," while
Hassan wants to "begin in the middle" and Mailer writes a
history which "inhabits a crazy house." There was a time
when the moving finger would write and having writ would
just move on. There was moreover a time when the moving
finger was coldly empirical. But then McLuhan came to
extinguish the Gutenburg galaxy, and Rowan and Martin
came to sock it to us. Now we also see through a shutter
brightly. Now the moving finger is psychedelic. And because
the brownian motion has moved us and the media that
would entertain us and the scholars that would inform us, it
is doubtful that we will ever be the same.

Afterword

The Social Utility of Popular Culture

I am reminded as I close these pages of a paraphrase
used by my fellow popculturalist Arthur Asa Berger in
opening his study of the comic strip character L'l
Abner: "They laughed," Berger wrote, "when I sat down at
the typewriter!" Even though the serious academic scrutiny
of American popular culture is well into its adolescence it is
still for very many within the academic community a
shallow calling. Thus the anthropologist who solemnly
analyzes authority in a Bengali village or the critic who
soberly explicates the rhymes of an obscure Mandarin poet
will each be seized by confusion, mirth, or disgust when
confronted with the careful analysis of a short story by *Good
Housekeeping* or a "Whopper" by Burger King. It is of little
moment that popular culture is the largest single fact of
American life and that as such it is of greater importance to
Americans than Bengali villages or Mandarin verse, for
such is the curious nature of the academic world.

However, it is not my intention in these final pages to
join the fracas either for or against the study of popular
culture. The trenches have been dug and labelled—"mid
cult," "mass cult," "mid-brow"—and the warriors are
welcome to the blood.[1] After all the popular culture can be
analyzed or ignored but it cannot be abolished. My text

rather, as this book closes, is a question: What is the social utility of popular culture, particularly within a democracy and particularly within the United States?

Democracy alas has become one of the looser terms, denoting now the town-meeting nature of government in ancient Athens and now the representative nature of government in the twentieth-century West and still now a mere catch word used to identify political systems as diverse as China and India, the United States and the Soviet Union, the United Kingdom and Yugoslavia. Still with *democracy* as with most words, if we do not mean what we say we usually know what we mean, and I have here in mind a definition that goes beyond patterns of American polity into the fabric of American society.

Perhaps *social democracy* is the appropriate phrase for it denotes that egalitarian aspect of society in the United States upon which foreign observers from before de Tocqueville to after James Bryce have remarked. It is this egalitarianism, this "equality of estimation" to use Lord Bryce's words, which sustains the average American's belief that individual persons deserve—even though they do not always receive—equality of treatment and equality of respect. And this "equality of estimation" is itself sustained by what the historian and popular culturist Russel Nye has called the "majority experience" in America, a national ethos and way of life that exhibits shared beliefs, attitudes, expectations, manners and customs. To be sure the American population is divisible into groups of region or ethnicity or income. But politically a democracy does not assign widely different levels of political authority to members of different groups and socially the various groups within a democracy should exhibit no remarkable variations in their lifestyles or "estimating," participating instead and for the most part in the "majority experience."

Americans themselves often ignore or deny their homogeneity. They prefer to alternately celebrate the diversity that distinguishes North Dakota wheat ranchers from New England housewives, and loathe the disparities that separate San Francisco broker from Alabama sharecropper. But when placed in a more cosmopolitan perspective—which of course is why the message of de Tocqueville and Bryce has usually come from abroad— America's diversities and disparities are more apparent than real. India for example can provide in a Bombay businessman, a Calcutta professor, a Kerala farmer, and a Kashmiri peddler persons who speak four different mother tongues, who wear four unique costumes and enjoy four unique cuisines, who represent four distinct genetic stocks and quite possibly worship four distinct deities. Yet through some curious political legerdemain they are fellow citizens of what is often billed as the largest democracy on earth. By contrast being an American is an astonishingly singular and unified experience.

Even when the homogeneity of America's "majority experience" is admitted however it still must be explained. The United States is not a traditional culture, a Polynesian island, say, whose cohesion is the accumulation of a history that stretches into time out of mind. Nor is it one of the many highly developed nations (of which Germany and Japan come to mind) whose cohesion is easily explained as the legacy of a shared past, society, culture. The United States is an invented nation, a land whose population is dense in its cultural origins, a people within whom the apocryphal native was the person who got off the boat before you did. How then has America, this potential babble of tongues, come to exhibit the cohesion that is an essential ingredient of a social democracy and perhaps of nationhood itself?

Customarily the answer to this question has been laid upon the altar of civil religion, and the theory is admittedly a compelling one. For while the American state is by law secular American law is by tradition spiritual. Hence the Declaration of Independence and the Constitution of the United States, once earthly documents of nation-building, have become religious scripture even as the Founding Fathers—along perhaps with Abraham Lincoln—have become the apostles. In any given historical moment, then, the leaders of state function not merely bureaucratically or politically but also ecclesiastically. In any given moment, also, the citizens are the saints, the defenders of the faith in war, its celebrants in peace, its communicants always. Thus what appears to be the culture's cohesion is in fact, so the theory goes, civil religion's orthodoxy.

But popular culturists like Bengali anthropologists and critics of Mandarin literature suspect a certain centrality in their subjects, and I for one am mindful that Mom's Apple Pie is not only an icon of the American civil religion but a registered trademark and an artifact of American popular culture. Apple pie and the Marlboro Man, celebrities, gasoline stations and hamburger stands, magazine fiction and magazines themselves, even the late (and, yes Canadian) Marshall McLuhan: these and the countless other elements of its popular culture contribute, I suspect, to the glue of American social democracy.

As an instrument of social cohesion popular culture in America is at least as old as Noah Webster's desire to build and sustain an American language, as old as James Fenimore Cooper's yen for an American literature, as old as Stephen Foster's urge for an American music. But it is in our own century that the popular culture's growth toward ubiquity has been most startling. That growth has of course been most clearly visible in the mass media. Television for instance has entered so many American homes that those without it are statistically insignificant, and the average American now watches television nearly thirty hours per week with any one of any season's top ten programs being viewed by at least twenty-five percent of the potential viewing audience. But the remainder of popular culture is also on display. Advertising, which the former semanticist Hayakawa once called the "largest single fact of our semantic environment," currently costs Americans forty-four billion dollars per year. Celebrities are everywhere, so much so that *People Magazine*, born in the mid-70s, already enjoyed a circulation of 2.3 million at decade's end. Vernacular architecture is equally ubiquitous: 200,000 service stations and 65,000 franchised eateries, to name only two of the many varieties. Mass magazines marshal equally impressive numbers: the highest circulation magazine in America today counts twenty million readers and no magazine among the top ten has a circulation not in excess of five million. And in the avenues of popular culture beyond these purviews it need perhaps only be pointed out that fewer than one hundred companies provide Americans with what they wear, eat and sit on. For better or worse the United States has become automobiles by Detroit (or Yokohoma, it matters not), clothing by Sears or Levi, books by Bantam, movies by Great Western, and ideas by Norman Peale or John Galbraith.

The social ultility of popular culture, then, is not to be measured merely in terms of entertainment or of the gratification of creature comforts, though to be sure it entertains and gratifies. The artifacts of popular culture are the agents of democratization, for better and for worse spreading farther and deeper into the population, "confirming," as Nye has written, "the majority experience."

Notes

Chapter One

[1]S. I. Hayakawa, "The Impact of Mass Media on Contemporary American Culture," a lecture delivered at Sacramento State College in 1960. Portions of the lecture, though not the anecdote, appear in *Language in Thought and Action,* 2nd ed. (New York, 1964), pp. 262-77.

[2]Leo Marx, *The Machine in the Garden* (New York, p. 4).

[3]The pertinent lore from Madison Avenue is available in trade journals as well as in an occasional popular magazine. See for instance Leo Burnett, "The Marlboro Story: How One of America's Most Popular Filter Cigarettes Got that Way," *New Yorker,* 34 (15 November 1958), 3; "Marlboro Won Success by Big Newspaper Ads," *Editor and Publisher,* 91 (6 December 1958), 26; "Saddlesoap, Please," *Advertising Age,* 31 (28 March 1960), 90; "Giant Size Remington Reproductions become Outdoor Boards, *ibid.,* 40 (20 January 1969), 32.

[4]John G. Cawelti, *Adventure, Mystery, and Romance* (Chicago, 1976), p. 193. Cawelti's earlier book *The Six-Gun Mystique* (Bowling Green, 1971) is also pertinent.

[5]Leslie A. Fiedler, "Montana, or the End of Jean-Jacques Rousseau," reprinted in *An End to Innocence* (Boston, 1955), p. 131.

[6]Marx, especially at p. 16.

[7]Marx similarly delineates the border of Arcadia: "One separates it from Rome, the other from the encroaching marshland." Within these borders the pastoral shepherd is "free of the repressions entailed by a complex civilization," but still "not prey to the violent uncertainties of nature." *Ibid.,* p. 22.

[8]Fiedler, pp. 134-35.

[9]Frederick Jackson Turner. "The Significance of the Frontier in American History," in *The Frontier in American History* (New York, 1920), p. 37.

[10]Fiedler, p. 135.

Chapter Two

[1]Tom Wolfe, *Radical Chic and Mau-Mauing the Flak Catcher* (New York, 1970).

[2]Hubert Saal, "Burt Bacharach, The Music Man 1970," *Newsweek,* 22 June 1970, pp. 50+. Other lore on Bacharach is available in such places as "Composer in Tartan Cap," *New Yorker,* 44 (21 December 1968), 27; "Musical Events," *ibid.,* 44 (18 January 1969), 84; Vincent Canby, "Ross Hunter's Version of 'Lost Horizon' Opens," *New York Times,* 15 March 1973, p. 58; Stephen Holden, "Dionne Warwick Makes Herself Over," *Rollng Stone,* 15 (November 1979, pp. 16+; and "Couples," *People,* 1 June 1981, pp. 82+.

[3]Orrin E. Klapp, "Hero Worship in America," *American Sociological Review,* 14 (1949), 54. Klapp's additional thoughts on the matter appear in *Heroes, Villains, and Fools* (Englewood Cliffs, 1962), and in *Symbolic Leaders* (Chicago, 1964).

[4]Klapp, "The Creation of Popular Heroes," *American Journal of Sociology,* 54 (1948), 135-41.

[5]See Daniel J. Boorstin, *The Image* (New York, 1961), especially pp. 3-6, 171-78.

[6]*Ibid.,* pp. 45-76, especially p. 57.

Chapter Three

[1]Christopher Tunnard and Henry Hope Reed, *American Skyline* (New York, 1953), pp. 15-31.

[2]Most of the data that appear here are from the Marathon Oil Company archives in Findlay, Ohio.

[5]John A. Kouwenhoven, *Made in America* (Garden City, 1948), p. 41. *Made in America* was subsequently republished as *The Arts in Modern American Civilization* (New York, 1967).

Chapter Four

[1]Much of the lore and detail that appears here is based on personal interviews with architects, planners, public relations officers, and other employees of Royal Castle Systems, Inc. or the Burger King Corporation. Foremost among them is Ray Taweel, dean of Burger King University, formerly known as Whopper College. However a few written sources are available, most notably Dunn and Bradstreet, *Million Dollar Directory,* 1975 (New York, 1974); "The Hamburger that Conquered the Country," *Time,* 17 (September 1973), pp. 84; Jan Cook, "The Hungry Fight for the Fast-Food Dollar," *Tropic,* 16 February 1973, pp. 6; R. Cherry, "Fast-Food Chains Expecting an Even Bigger Bit of Sales," *New York Times,* 5 January 1977, p. D5; "Burger King in Orient," *ibid.,* 8 August 1979; and *ibid.,* 23 July 1980, p. D2.

[2]Reyner Banham, *Los Angeles: The Architecture of Four Ecologies* (New York, 1971), pp. 118-20.

[3]Robert Venturi, *et al., Learning from Las Vegas* (Cambridge, 1972), p. 64.

[4]Kouwenhoven, p. 41.

[5]Siegfried Giedion, *Mechanization Takes Command* (New York, 1948), pp. 31-32.

Chapter Five

[1]Frank Luther Mott, *A History of American Magazines* (Cambridge, 1938-68), V, 143.

[2]See Vladimir Propp, *Morphology of the Folktale,* 2nd ed. (Austin, 1968), and Claude Levi-Strauss, "The Structural Study of Myth," *Journal of American Folklore,* 68 (1955), 428-44, especially 435.

[3]Hugh Cave, "To Trust in Andy," *Good Housekeeping,* April, 1965, pp. 102.

[4]On linear structure see Alan Dundes, "Introduction to the Second Edition," in Propp, pp. xi-xvii.

[5]See Dundes.

[6]Cave, "Double Wedding," *Good Housekeeping,* July, 1965, pp. 88.

[7]Data regarding *Good Housekeeping's,* readership during the period are from W.R. Simmons, "Standard Magazine Audience Report, Selected Characteristics of Adult Female Reader's" 1972.

[8]R.W. Alexander, "The Short Short Story," *Writer,* 80 (August, 1967), 18.

[9]Cora DuBois, "The Dominant Value Profile of American Culture," *American Anthropologist,* 62 (1955), 1233.

[10]Alexander, "My Young and Truly Love," *Good Housekeeping,* October, 1966, pp. 102.

Chapter Six

[1]Harvey Cox, "Playboy's Doctrine of Male," *Christianity and Crisis,* 21 (17 April 1961), 57.

[2][Editors], *Playboy,* 1 (December, 1953), [3].

[3]*Ibid.,* 6 (October, 1959), 38.

[4]Hugh M. Hefner, "The Playboy Philosophy," *Ibid.,* 9 (December, 1962), 73.

[5]*Ibid.,* 10 (January, 1963), 51.

[6]"Playboy's Political Preference Chart," *ibid.,* 17 (November, 1970), 184.+

[7]Cox, 57.

[8]Benjamin DeMott, "The Anatomy of 'Playboy,' " *Commentary,* 34 (August, 1962), 112.

[5]Peter Schrag, *The Decline of the Wasp* (New York, 1971), pp. 185-225, especially pp. 198-99.

Chapter Seven

[1]Christopher Ricks, in *McLuhan: Hot and Cool,* ed. G.E. Stearn (New York, 1967), pp. 211-27.

[2]Marshall McLuhan, *Understanding Media* (New York, 1964), pp. 25-26.

[3]Allan Nevins, *The Gateway to History* (Chicago, 1938, 1963), p. 14.

[4]McLuhan, *The Mechanical Bridge* (New York, 1951), pp. 3-4.

[5]"Playboy Interview: Marshall McLuhan," *Playboy,* 16 (March, 1969), 53+.

[6]Ihab Hassan, "Frontiers of Criticism: Metaphors of Silence," *Viriginia Quarterly Review,* 46 (1970), 87.

[7]Hassan, "Silence, Revolution, and Consciousness," *Massachusetts Review,* 10 (1969), 461, 472.

[8]Norman Mailer, *The Armies of the Night* (New York, 1968), pp. 65-66.

[9]Neil Postman and Charles Weingartner, *Teaching as a Subversive Activity* (New York, 1969), especially 23, 29, 35.

Afterword

[1]See Russel Nye, *The Unembarrassed Muse* (New York, 1970), especially pp. 417-20 for a primer on the debate.

Dr. Lohof received his education at Stetson University and Syracuse University. He has taught at Heidelberg College in Ohio and was chair of the History Department at the University of Miami, Coral Gables, Florida for several years.

Dr. Lohof was director of the American Studies Research Centre in Hyderabad, India. At present he is with the United States Educational Foundation, Islamabad, Pakistan.